The
COMPLETE
VICTORIAN
TREASURY

Sheila Pickles

PAVILION

CONTENTS

DEDICATED TO PETER J. HALL

Celebrating a lifetime of friendship

Introduction

Dear Reader,

Selecting the pieces for this anthology has been a pleasure, for many of them recall experiences from my own lifetime.

First of all the state of being in love is like none other, as David Copperfield finds out; it causes us to lose all sense of perspective, as Anna Karenina shows, and often brings grief to our families, like Shakespeare's heroines Juliet and Jessica. Unrequited love is the saddest state of all – for both those who have been rejected and those who have not yet dared to reach out their hands. Heathcliff was to turn almost bestial with jealousy and bitterness at Cathy's marriage to Edgar Linton, and Mr. Rochester was driven to commit bigamy in order to marry Jane Eyre.

Marriage has been celebrated in many novels and poems. My anthology *Bridal Bouquet* celebrates throughout literature, relationships between humble cottagers, lords and ladies, princes and princesses. All progressed through the crescendo of courtship and engagement towards the final happy ending of an announcement of marriage, and the wedding.

The Grand Tour originated in the eighteenth century when the children of wealthy families were sent to Europe to finish their education, to study the Arts and widen their horizons or simply to honeymoon following a marriage. The Romantic poets, Byron, Shelley, Keats and Browning then discovered the joys of the Mediterranean and wrote widely of Italy and Greece, which similarly attracted American writers and artists, such as Mark Twain and Henry James. The result was that in Victorian times a European Tour became as fashionable for Americans as the British. The tales are so numerous and the opinions so varied that it has been hard to make a selection which both informs and entertains. I hope my final choice will inspire others on their travels.

My earliest memories are of my mother singing 'Golden Slumbers' to me in the nursery, and my sister and I can still recite the poems of A. A. Milne and Robert Louis Stevenson that our mother used to read to us. Sharing stories and poems with a child is wonderfully rewarding and opens the door to reading, which is a gift for life and which I have collected here under the heading *Mother and Child*.

Above all Christmas is a time for children and it brings out the child in all of us. As I grew up, Christmas Day itself became something of an anticlimax. Perhaps this is because children nowadays have high expectations of Christmas. Interesting too that almost one hundred years ago George Bernard Shaw was rebelling against Christmas for its insincerity and vulgarity. Dickens wrote that a man must be a misanthrope if he does not feel some joviality at the recurrence of Christmas and I would say that it is a poor-spirited creature indeed who feels no emotion at hearing the time-worn carols or finding a silver sixpence in his pudding.

This *Complete Victorian Treasury* combines all the above themes that were so important for our forebears and which retain a timeless significance for all contemporary lives.

Sheila Pickles, 1999

LOVE

❧ Summer Night ❧

Now sleeps the crimson petal, now the white;
Nor waves the cypress in the palace walk;
Nor winks the gold fin in the porphyry font:
The firefly wakens: waken thou with me.

Now droops the milk-white peacock like a ghost,
And like a ghost she glimmers on to me.

Now lies the Earth all Danaë to the stars,
And all thy heart lies open unto me.

Now slides the silent meteor on, and leaves
A shining furrow, as thy thoughts in me.

Now folds the lily all her sweetness up,
And slips into the bosom of the lake:
So fold thyself, my dearest, thou, and slip
Into my bosom and be lost in me.

LORD TENNYSON, 1809–1892

◆ Romeo and Juliet ◆

BUT soft, what light through yonder window breaks?
It is the east, and Juliet is the sun.
Arise, fair sun, and kill the envious moon.
Who is already sick and pale with grief
That thou, her maid, art far more fair than she.
Be not her maid, since she is envious.
Her vestal livery is but sick and green,
And none but fools do wear it; cast it off.
    [*Enter Juliet aloft*]
It is my lady, O, it is my love.
O that she knew she were!
She speaks, yet she says nothing. What of that?
Her eye discourses; I will answer it.
I am too bold. 'Tis not to me she speaks.
Two of the fairest stars in all the heaven,
Having some business, do entreat her eyes
To twinkle in their spheres till they return.
What if her eyes were there, they in her head?—

The brightness of her cheek would shame those stars
As daylight doth a lamp; her eye in heaven
Would through the airy region stream so bright
That birds would sing and think it were not night.
See how she leans her cheek upon her hand.
O, that I were a glove upon that hand,
That I might touch that cheek!

Juliet Ay me.

Romeo [*aside*] She speaks.
O, speak again, bright angel; for thou art
As glorious to this night, being o'er my head,
As is a wingèd messenger of heaven
Unto the white upturnèd wond'ring eyes
Of mortals that fall back to gaze on him
When he bestrides the lazy-passing clouds
And sails upon the bosom of the air.

Juliet [*not knowing Romeo hears her*]
O Romeo, Romeo, wherefore art thou Romeo?
Deny thy father and refuse thy name,
Or if thou wilt not, be but sworn my love,
And I'll no longer be a Capulet.

Romeo [*aside*]
Shall I hear more, or shall I speak at this?

Juliet
'Tis but thy name that is my enemy.
Thou art thyself, though not a Montague.
What's Montague? It is nor hand, nor foot,
Nor arm, nor face, nor any other part
Belonging to a man. O, be some other name!
What's in a name? That which we call a rose
By any other word would smell as sweet.
So Romeo would, were he not Romeo called,
Retain that dear perfection which he owes
Without that title. Romeo, doff thy name,
And for thy name—which is no part of thee—
Take all myself.

WILLIAM SHAKESPEARE, 1564–1616

— 15 —

Algernon [*speaking very rapidly*]: Cecily, ever since I first looked upon your wonderful and incomparable beauty, I have dared to love you wildly, passionately, devotedly, hopelessly.

Cecily: I don't think that you should tell me that you love me wildly, passionately, devotedly, hopelessly. Hopelessly doesn't seem to make much sense, does it?

Algernon: Cecily! . . .

. . . I don't care for anybody in the whole world but you. I love you, Cecily. You will marry me, won't you?

Cecily: You silly boy! Of course. Why, we have been engaged for the last three months.

Algernon: For the last three months?

Cecily: Yes, it will be exactly three months on Thursday.

Algernon: But how did we become engaged?

Cecily: Well, ever since dear Uncle Jack first confessed to us that he had a younger brother who was very wicked and bad, you, of course, have formed the chief topic of conversation between myself and Miss Prism. And, of course, a man who is much talked about is always very attractive. One feels there must be something in him, after all. I dare say it was foolish of me, but I fell in love with you, Ernest.

Algernon: Darling. And when was the engagement actually settled?

Cecily: On the 14th of February last. Worn out by your entire ignorance of my existence, I determined to end the matter one way or the other, and after a long struggle with myself I accepted you under this dear old tree here. The next day I bought this little ring in your name, and this is the little bangle with the true lovers' knot I promised you always to wear.

Algernon: Did I give you this? It's very pretty, isn't it?

Cecily: Yes, you've wonderfully good taste, Ernest. It's the excuse I've always given for your leading such a bad life. And this is the box in which I keep all your dear letters. [*Kneels at table, opens box, and produces letters tied up with blue ribbon.*]

Algernon: My letters! But, my own sweet Cecily, I have never written you any letters.

Cecily: You need hardly remind me of that, Ernest. I remember only too well that I was forced to write your letters for you. I wrote always three times a week, and sometimes oftener.

Algernon: Oh, do let me read them, Cecily?

Cecily: Oh, I couldn't possibly. They would make you far too conceited. [*Replaces box.*] The three you wrote me after I had broken off the engagement are so beautiful, and so badly spelled, that even now I can hardly read them without crying a little.

Algernon: But was our engagement ever broken off?

Cecily: Of course it was. On the 22nd of last March. You can see the entry if you like. [*Shows diary.*] "To-day I broke off my engagement with Ernest. I feel it is better to do so. The weather still continues charming."

Algernon: But why on earth did you break it off? What had I done? I had done nothing at all. Cecily, I am very much hurt indeed to hear you broke it off. Particularly when the weather was so charming.

Cecily: It would hardly have been a really serious engagement if it hadn't been broken off at least once. But I forgave you before the week was out.

Oscar Wilde, 1854–1900

— 18 —

🌿 *Wanton Maidens* 🌿

THE wanton Maidens him espying, stood
   Gazing a while at his vnwonted guise;
Then th'one her selfe low ducked in the flood,
Abasht, that her a straunger did avise:
But th'other rather higher did arise,
And her two lilly paps aloft displayd,
And all, that might his melting hart entise
To her delights, she vnto him bewrayd:
The rest hid vnderneath, him more desirous made.

FAERIE QUEEN, EDMUND SPENSER, 1552–1599

Lorenzo and Jessica

Lorenzo The moon shines bright. In such a night as this,
When the sweet wind did gently kiss the trees,
And they did make no noise—in such a night,
Troilus methinks mounted the Troyan walls,
And sigh'd his soul toward the Grecian tents,
Where Cressid lay that night.

Jessica In such a night
Did Thisby fearfully o'ertrip the dew,
And saw the lion's shadow ere himself,
And ran dismayed away.

Lorenzo In such a night
Stood Dido with a willow in her hand
Upon the wild sea-banks, and waft her love
To come again to Carthage.

Jessica In such a night
Medea gathered the enchanted herbs
That did renew old Æson.

Lorenzo In such a night
Did Jessica steal from the wealthy Jew,
And with an unthrift love did run from Venice
As far as Belmont.

Jessica In such a night
Did young Lorenzo swear he lov'd her well,
Stealing her soul with many vows of faith,
And ne'er a true one.

Lorenzo In such a night
Did pretty Jessica, like a little shrew,
Slander her love, and he forgave it her.

THE MERCHANT OF VENICE, WILLIAM SHAKESPEARE, 1564–1616

The Sun Rising

Busy old fool, unruly Sun,
 Why dost thou thus,
Through windows, and through curtains, call on us?
Must to thy motions lovers' seasons run?
  Saucy pedantic wretch, go chide
  Late school-boys and sour prentices,
  Go tell Court-huntsmen that the King will ride,
  Call country ants to harvest offices;
Love, all alike, no season knows nor clime,
Nor hours, days, months, which are the rags of time.

  Thy beams so reverend and strong
  Why shouldst thou think?
I could eclipse and cloud them with a wink,
But that I would not lose her sight so long.
  If her eyes have not blinded thine,
  Look, and to-morrow late tell me,
  Whether both th'Indias of spice and mine
  Be where thou left'st them, or lie here with me.
Ask for those kings whom thou saw'st yesterday.
And thou shalt hear, "All here in one bed lay."

  She's all states, and all princes I;
  Nothing else is;
Princes do but play us; compar'd to this,
All honour's mimic, all wealth alchemy.
  Thou sun art half as happy as we,
  In that the world's contracted thus;
  Thine age asks ease, and since thy duties be
To warm the world, that's done in warming us.
Shine here to us, and thou art everywhere;
This bed thy centre is, these walls, thy sphere.

JOHN DONNE. 1572–1631

⸘ The Rose Did Caper ⸙

THE Rose did caper on her cheek—
Her Bodice rose and fell—
Her pretty speech—like drunken men—
Did stagger pitiful—

Her fingers fumbled at her work—
Her needle would not go—
What ailed so smart a little Maid—
It puzzled me to know—

Till opposite—I spied a cheek
That bore *another* Rose—
Just opposite—Another speech
That like the Drunkard goes—

A Vest that like her Bodice, danced—
To the immortal tune—
Till those two troubled—little Clocks
Ticked softly into one.

EMILY DICKINSON. 1830–1886

✥ The Disciple ✥

WHEN Narcissus died the pool of his pleasure changed from a cup of sweet waters into a cup of salt tears, and the Oreads came weeping through the woodland that they might sing to the pool and give it comfort.

And when they saw that the pool had changed from a cup of sweet waters into a cup of salt tears, they loosened the green tresses of their hair and cried to the pool and said, "We do not wonder that you should mourn in this manner for Narcissus, so beautiful was he."

"But was Narcissus beautiful?" said the pool.

"Who should know that better than you?" answered the Oreads. "Us did he ever pass by, but you he sought for, and would lie on your banks and look down at you, and in the mirror of your waters he would mirror his own beauty."

And the pool answered, "But I loved Narcissus because, as he lay on my banks and looked down at me, in the mirror of his eyes I saw ever my own beauty mirrored.

OSCAR WILDE. 1854–1900

Love

ALL thoughts, all passions, all delights,
    Whatever stirs this mortal frame,
All are but ministers of Love,
    And feed his sacred flame.

Oft in my waking dreams do I
Live o'er again that happy hour,
When midway on the mount I lay,
    Beside the ruin'd tower.

The moonshine, stealing o'er the scene,
Had blended with the lights of eve;
And she was there, my hope, my joy,
    My own dear Genevieve!

She lean'd against the armèd man,
The statue of the armèd Knight;
She stood and listen'd to my lay,
    Amid the lingering light . . . .

She half enclosed me with her arms,
She press'd me with a meek embrace;
And bending back her head, look'd up,
    And gazed upon my face.

'Twas partly love, and partly fear,
And partly 'twas a bashful art,
That I might rather feel, than see,
    The swelling of her heart.

I calm'd her fears, and she was calm,
And told her love with virgin pride;
And so I won my Genevieve,
    My bright and beauteous Bride.

LOVE. SAMUEL TAYLOR COLERIDGE. 1772–1834

❧ Holiday Gown ❧

In holiday gown, and my new-fangled hat,
    Last Monday I tripped to the fair;
I held up my head, and I'll tell you for what,
    Brisk Roger I guessed would be there:
He woos me to marry whenever we meet,
    There's honey sure dwells on his tongue!
He hugs me so close, and he kisses so sweet,
    I'd wed – if I were not too young.

Fond Sue, I'll assure you, laid hold on the boy,
    (The vixen would fain be his bride)
Some token she claimed, either ribbon or toy,
    And swore that she'd not be denied:
A top-knot he bought her, and garters of green,
    Pert Susan was cruelly stung;
I hate her so much, that, to kill her with spleen,
    I'd wed – if I were not too young.

He whispered such soft pretty things in mine ear!
    He flattered, he promised, and swore!
Such trinkets he gave me, such laces and gear,
    That, trust me, – my pockets ran o'er:
Some ballads he bought me, the best he could find,
    And sweetly their burthen he sung;
Good faith! he's so handsome, so witty, and kind,
    I'd wed – if I were not too young.

The sun was just setting, 'twas time to retire,
    (Our cottage was distant a mile)
I rose to be gone – Roger bowed like a squire,
    And handed me over the stile:
His arms he threw round me – love laughed in his eye,
    He led me the meadows among,
There pressed me so close, I agreed, with a sigh,
    To wed – for I was not too young.

JOHN CUNNINGHAM, 1729–1773

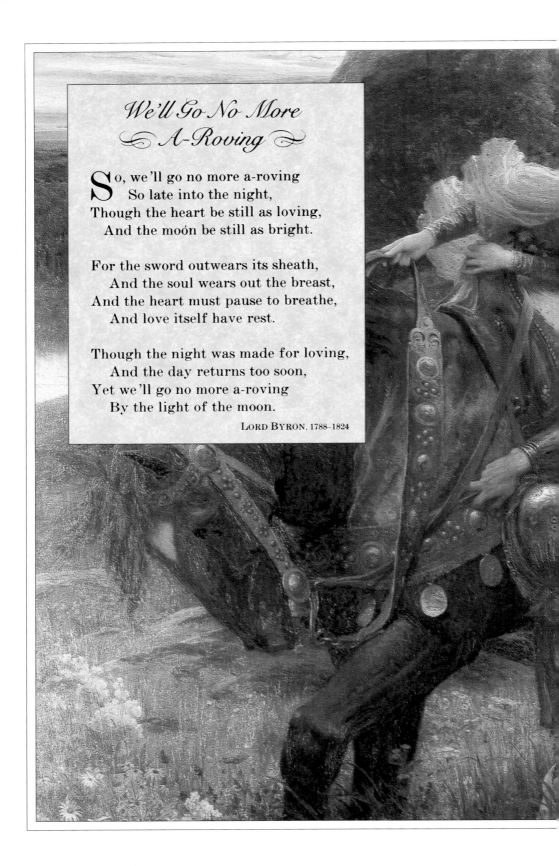

We'll Go No More
A-Roving

So, we'll go no more a-roving
  So late into the night,
Though the heart be still as loving,
  And the moon be still as bright.

For the sword outwears its sheath,
  And the soul wears out the breast,
And the heart must pause to breathe,
  And love itself have rest.

Though the night was made for loving,
  And the day returns too soon,
Yet we'll go no more a-roving
  By the light of the moon.

LORD BYRON, 1788–1824

✦ Meg in Love ✦

MEG meanwhile had apparently forgotten the matter, and was absorbed in preparations for her father's return; but all of a sudden a change seemed to come over her, and, for a day or two, she was quite unlike herself. She started when spoken to, blushed when looked at, was very quiet, and sat over her sewing, with a timid, troubled look on her face. To her mother's inquiries she answered that she was quite well, and Jo's she silenced by begging to be let alone.

"She feels it in the air–love, I mean–and she's going very fast. She's got most of the symptoms,–is twittery and cross, doesn't eat, lies awake, and mopes in corners. I caught her singing that song he gave her, and once she said 'John,' as you do, and then turned as red as a poppy. Whatever shall we do?" said Jo, looking ready for any measures, however violent.

"Nothing but wait. Let her alone, be kind and patient, and father's coming will settle everything," replied her mother.

LITTLE WOMEN, LOUISA MAY ALCOTT, 1832–1888

Cathy and Heathcliff

You teach me how cruel you've been—cruel and false. Why did you despise me? Why did you betray your own heart, Cathy? I have not one word of comfort. You deserve this. You have killed yourself. Yes, you may kiss me, and cry, and wring out my kisses and tears; they'll blight you—they'll damn you. You loved me; then what right had you to leave me? What right—answer me—for the poor fancy you felt for Linton? Because misery, and degradation, and death, and nothing that God or Satan could inflict would have parted us, you, of your own free will, did it. I have not broken your heart—you have broken it; and in breaking it you have broken mine. So much the worse for me that I am strong. Do I want to live? What kind of living will it be, when you—O God—would you like to live with your soul in the grave?

WUTHERING HEIGHTS, EMILY BRONTË, 1818–1848

Modern Love

AND what is love? It is a doll dress'd up
For idleness to cosset, nurse, and dandle;
A thing of soft misnomers, so divine
That silly youth doth think to make itself
Divine by loving, and so goes on
Yawning and doting a whole summer long,
Till Miss's comb is made a pearl tiara,
And common Wellingtons turn Romeo boots;
Then Cleopatra lives at number seven,
And Antony resides in Brunswick Square.
Fools! if some passions high have warm'd the world,
If Queens and Soldiers have play'd deep for hearts,
It is no reason why such agonies
Should be more common than the growth of weeds.
Fools! make me whole again that weighty pearl
The Queen of Egypt melted, and I'll say
That ye may love in spite of beaver hats.

JOHN KEATS, 1795–1821

Perfect Woman

S HE was a phantom of delight
  When first she gleam'd upon my sight;
A lovely apparition, sent
To be a moment's ornament;
Her eyes as stars of twilight fair;
Like twilight's, too, her dusky hair;
But all things else about her drawn
From May-time and the cheerful dawn;
A dancing shape, an image gay,
To haunt, to startle, and waylay.

I saw her upon nearer view,
A Spirit, yet a Woman too!
Her household motions light and free,
And steps of virgin liberty;
A countenance in which did meet
Sweet records, promises as sweet;
A creature not too bright or good
For human nature's daily food;
For transient sorrows, simple wiles,
Praise, blame, love, kisses, tears, and smiles.

And now I see with eye serene
The very pulse of the machine;
A being breathing thoughtful breath,
A traveller between life and death;
The reason firm, the temperate will,
Endurance, foresight, strength, and skill;
A perfect Woman, nobly plann'd,
To warn, to comfort, and command;
And yet a Spirit still, and bright
With something of angelic light.

WILLIAM WORDSWORTH. 1770–1850

❧ Sonnet ❧

L ET me not to the marriage of true minds
  Admit impediments. Love is not love
Which alters when it alteration finds,
Or bends with the remover to remove:
O, no! it is an ever-fixed mark.
That looks on tempests and is never shaken;
It is the star to every wand'ring bark,
Whose worth's unknown, although his height be taken.
Love's not Time's fool, though rosy lips and cheeks
Within his bending sickle's compass come;
Love alters not with his brief hours and weeks,
But bears it out even to the edge of doom:—
    If this be error and upon me proved,
    I never writ, nor no man ever loved.

WILLIAM SHAKESPEARE, 1564–1616

How Do I Love Thee?

PORTUGUESE SONNET

How do I love thee: Let me count the ways.
I love thee to the depth and breadth and height
My soul can reach, when feeling out of sight
For the ends of Being and ideal Grace.
I love thee to the level of every day's
Most quiet need, by sun and candlelight.
I love thee freely, as men strive for Right;
I love thee purely, as they turn from Praise.
I love thee with the passion put to use
In my old griefs, and with my childhood's faith.
I love thee with a love I seemed to lose
With my lost saints,–I love thee with the breath,
Smiles, tears, of all my life!–and, if God choose,
I shall but love thee better after death.

ELIZABETH BARRETT BROWNING, 1806–1861

✒ Of Love and Champagne ✑

THEY sat down to table, and the waiter having handed the wine card to Forestier, Madame de Marelle exclaimed: "Give these gentlemen whatever they like, but for us iced champagne, the best, sweet champagne."

The Ostend oysters were brought in, tiny and plump, like little ears enclosed in shells, and melting between the tongue and the palate like salted bon-bons. Then, after the soup, a trout was served, as rose-tinted as a young girl, and the guests began to talk.

They spoke at first of a current scandal and then they began to talk of love. Without admitting it to be eternal, Duroy understood it as enduring, creating a bond, a tender friendship, a confidence. The union of the senses was only a seal to the union of hearts. But he was angry at the outrageous jealousies, melodramatic scenes and unpleasantnesses which almost always accompany ruptures.

When he ceased speaking, Madame de Marelle replied: "Yes, it is the only good thing in life, and we often spoil it by preposterous unreasonableness."

Madame Forestier, who was toying with her knife, added: "Yes – yes – it is pleasant to be loved."

And she seemed to be carrying her dream farther, to be thinking things that she dared not give words to.

As the first entrée was slow in coming, they sipped from time to time a mouthful of champagne and nibbled bits of crust. And the thought of love slowly intoxicated their souls, as the bright wine, rolling drop by drop down their throats, fired their blood and perturbed their minds.

The waiter brought in some lamb cutlets, delicate and tender, upon a thick layer of asparagus tips.

"Ah! this is good," exclaimed Forestier; and they ate slowly, enjoying the delicate meal and the vegetables as smooth as cream.

Duroy resumed: "For my part, when I love a woman, everything in the world disappears." He said this in a tone of conviction.

Madame Forestier murmured in accents of indifference: "There is no happiness comparable to that of the first hand-clasp, when the one asks: 'Do you love me?' and the other replies, 'Yes'."

BEL AMI. GUY DE MAUPASSANT. 1850–1893

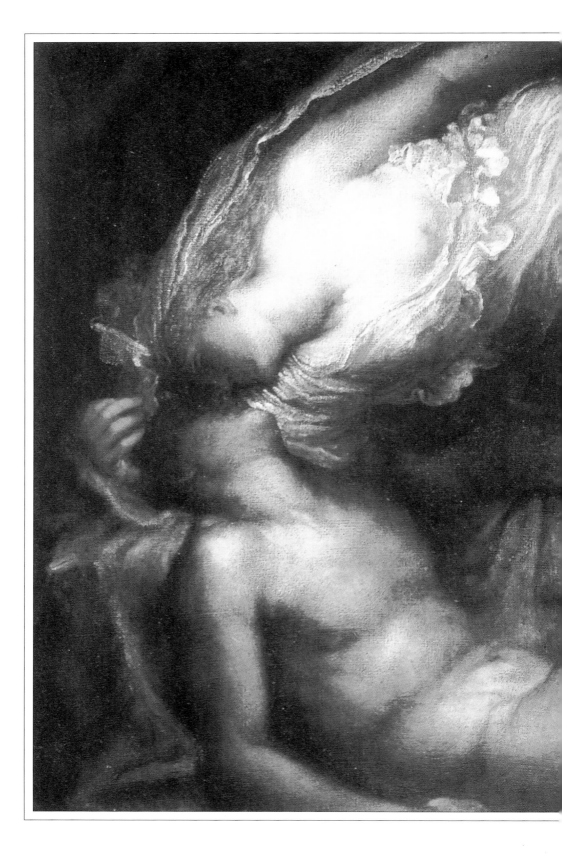

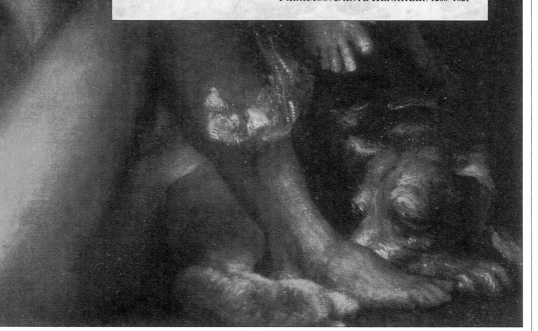

 **Divine Love**

FROM CANTO XXXIII

O LIGHT Eternal, that alone abidest in Thyself, alone knowest Thyself, and, known to Thyself and knowing, lovest and smilest on Thyself! That circling which, thus begotten, appeared in Thee as reflected light, when my eyes dwelt on it for a time, seemed to me, within it and in its own colour, painted with our likeness, for which my sight was wholly given to it. Like the geometer who sets all his mind to the squaring of the circle and for all his thinking does not discover the principle he needs, such was I at that strange sight. I wished to see how the image was fitted to the circle and how it has its place there; but my own wings were not sufficient for that, had not my mind been smitten by a flash wherein came its wish. Here power failed the high phantasy; but now my desire and will, like a wheel that spins with even motion, were revolved by the Love that moves the sun and the other stars.

PARADISO. DANTE ALIGHIERI, 1265–1321

BRIDAL BOUQUET

A SINGLE MAN

*I*T IS a truth universally acknowledged, that a single man in possession of a good fortune must be in want of a wife.

However little known the feelings or views of such a man may be on his first entering a neighbourhood, this truth is so well fixed in the minds of the surrounding families, that he is considered as the rightful property of someone or other of their daughters.

"My dear Mr. Bennet," said his lady to him one day, "have you heard that Netherfield Park is let at last?"

Mr. Bennet replied that he had not.

"But it is," returned she, "for Mrs. Long has just been here, and she told me all about it."

"Do not you want to know who has taken it?" cried his wife impatiently.

"*You* want to tell me, and I have no objection to hearing it."

"Why, my dear, you must know. Mrs. Long says that Netherfield is taken by a young man of large fortune from the north of England; that he came down on Monday in a chaise and four to see the place, and was so much delighted with it, that he agreed with Mr. Morris immediately; that he is to take possession before Michaelmas, and some of his servants are to be in the house by the end of next week."

"What is his name?"

"Bingley."

"Is he married or single?"

"Oh! single, my dear, to be sure! A single man of large fortune; four or five thousand a year. What a fine thing for our girls!"

"How so? How can it affect them?"

"My dear Mr. Bennet," replied his wife, "how can you be so tiresome! You must know that I am thinking of his marrying one of them."

FROM *PRIDE AND PREJUDICE* BY JANE AUSTEN, 1775-1817

INNOCENCE

OROTHEA, with all her eagerness to know the truths of life, retained very childlike ideas about marriage. She felt sure that she would have accepted the judicious Hooker, if she had been born in time to save him from that wretched mistake he made in matrimony; or John Milton when his blindness had come on; or any of the other great men whose odd habits it would have been glorious piety to endure; but an amiable handsome baronet, who said "Exactly" to her remarks even when she expressed uncertainty, – how could he affect her as a lover? The really delightful marriage must be that where your husband was a sort of father, and could teach you even Hebrew, if you wished it. . . .

And how should Dorothea not marry? – a girl so handsome and with such prospects? Nothing could hinder it but her love of extremes, and her insistence on regulating life according to notions which might cause a wary man to hesitate before he made her an offer, or even might lead her at last to refuse all offers. A young lady of some birth and fortune, who knelt suddenly down on a brick floor by the side of a sick labourer and prayed fervidly as if she thought herself living in the time of the Apostles – who had strange whims of fasting like a Papist, and of sitting up at night to read old theological books! Such a wife might awaken you some fine morning with a new scheme for the application of her income which would interfere with political economy and the keeping of saddle-horses: a man would naturally think twice before he risked himself in such fellowship. Women were expected to have weak opinions; but the great safeguard of society and of domestic life was, that opinions were not acted on. Sane people did what their neighbours did, so that if any lunatics were at large, one might know and avoid them.

FROM *MIDDLEMARCH* BY GEORGE ELIOT, 1819-1880

THE BRACELET TO JULIA

WHY I tye about thy wrist,
  Julia, this my silken twist;
  For what other reason is 't,
But to shew thee how in part
Thou my pretty captive art?
But thy bond-slave is my heart;
'Tis but silke that bindeth thee.

Knap the thread and thou art free;
But 'tis otherwise with me;
I am bound, and fast bound so,
That from thee I cannot go;
If I co'd, I wo'd not so.

ROBERT HERRICK, 1591-1674

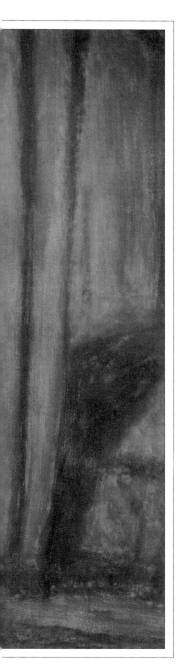

THE EVE OF ST. AGNES

*F*ULL on this casement shone the wintry moon,
  And threw warm gules on Madeline's fair breast,
    As down she knelt for heaven's grace and boon;
Rose-bloom fell on her hands, together prest,
And on her silver cross soft amethyst,
And on her hair a glory, like a saint:
She seem'd a splendid angel, newly drest,
Save wings, for heaven: – Porphyro grew faint:
She knelt, so pure a thing, so free from mortal taint.

Anon his heart revives: her vespers done,
Of all its wreathed pearls her hair she frees;
Unclasps her warmed jewels one by one;
Loosens her fragrant bodice; by degrees
Her rich attire creeps rustling to her knees:
Half-hidden, like a mermaid in sea-weed,
Pensive awhile she dreams awake, and sees,
In fancy, fair St. Agnes in her bed,
But dares not look behind, or all the charm is fled.

"My Madeline! sweet dreamer! lovely bride!
Say, may I be for aye thy vassal blest?
Thy beauty's shield, heart-shaped and vermeil dyed?
Ah, silver shrine, here will I take my rest
After so many hours of toil and quest,
A famish'd pilgrim, – saved by miracle.
Though I have found, I will not rob thy nest
Saving of thy sweet self; if thou think'st well
To trust, fair Madeline, to no rude infidel.

JOHN KEATS, 1795-1821

CATHERINE IN LOVE

ETWEEN the end of March, when these things happened, and the end of April, when Catherine married
Christopher, all taxi-drivers, bus-conductors and
railway-porters called her Miss.

Such was the effect Christopher had on her. Except for
him, she reflected, they probably would have addressed her
as Mother, for except for him she would have been profound-
ly miserable at this time, in the deep disgrace and pain of
being cut off from Virginia, from whom her letters came
back unopened, re-addressed by Stephen; and there was
nothing like inward misery, she knew, for turning women
into apparent mothers, old mothers, just as there was nothing
like inward happiness for turning them into apparent misses,
young misses. She had this inward happiness, for she had
Christopher to love her, to comfort her, to feed her with sweet
names; and she flowered in his warmth into a beauty she had
never possessed in the tepid days of George. Obviously what
the world needed was love. She couldn't help thinking this
when she caught sight of her own changed face in the glass.

FROM *LOVE* BY ELIZABETH VON ARNIM, 1866-1941

A FEW days after the engagement was announced Mrs. Honeychurch made Lucy and her Fiasco come to a little garden party in the neighbourhood, for naturally she wanted to show people that her daughter was marrying a presentable man.

Cecil was more than presentable; he looked distinguished, and it was very pleasant to see his slim figure keeping step with Lucy, and his long, fair face responding when Lucy spoke to him. People congratulated Mrs. Honeychurch, which is, I believe, a social blunder, but it pleased her, and she introduced Cecil rather indiscriminately to some stuffy dowagers.

At tea a misfortune took place: a cup of coffee was upset over Lucy's figured silk, and though Lucy feigned indifference her mother feigned nothing of the sort, but dragged her indoors to have the frock treated by a sympathetic maid. They were gone some time, and Cecil was left with the dowagers. When they returned he was not as pleasant as he had been.

"Do you go to much of this sort of thing?" he asked when they were driving home.

"Oh, now and then," said Lucy, who had rather enjoyed herself.

"Is it typical of county society?"

"I suppose so. Mother, would it be?"

"Plenty of society," said Mrs. Honeychurch, who was trying to remember the hang of one of the dresses.

Seeing that her thoughts were elsewhere, Cecil bent towards Lucy and said:

"To me it seemed perfectly appalling, disastrous, portentous."

"I am so sorry that you were stranded."

"Not that, but the congratulations. It is so disgusting, the way an engagement is regarded as public property – a kind of waste place where every outsider may shoot his vulgar sentiment. All those old women smirking!"

"One has to go through it, I suppose. They won't notice us so much next time."

"But my point is that their whole attitude is wrong. An engagement – horrid word in the first place – is a private matter, and should be treated as such."

Yet the smirking old women, however wrong individually, were racially correct. The spirit of the generations had smiled through them, rejoicing in the engagement of Cecil and Lucy because it promised the continuance of life on earth. To Cecil and Lucy it promised something quite different – personal love. Hence Cecil's irritation and Lucy's belief that his irritation was just.

"How tiresome!" she said. "Couldn't you have escaped to tennis?"

FROM *A ROOM WITH A VIEW* BY E.M. FORSTER, 1879-1970

ISABEL'S CHOICE

"*W*HY shouldn't I like Mr. Osmond, since others have done so?"

"Others, at their wildest moments, never wanted to marry him. There's nothing *of* him," Mrs. Touchett explained.

"Then he can't hurt me," said Isabel.

"Do you think you're going to be happy? No one's happy, in such doings, you should know."

"I shall set the fashion then. What does one marry for?"

"What *you* will marry for, heaven only knows. People usually marry as they go into partnership – to set up a house. But in your partnership you'll bring everything."

"Is it that Mr. Osmond isn't rich? Is that what you're talking about?" Isabel asked.

"He has no money; he has no name; he has no importance. I value such things and I have the courage to say it; I think they're very precious. Many other people think the same, and they show it. But they give some other reason."

Isabel hesitated a little. "I think I value everything that's valuable. I care very much for money, and that's why I wish Mr. Osmond to have a little."

"Give it to him then; but marry someone else."

FROM *THE PORTRAIT OF A LADY* BY HENRY JAMES. 1843-1916

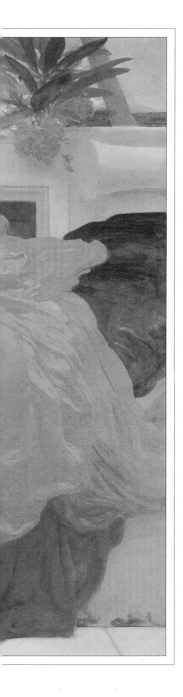

MARRIAGE MORNING

*L*IGHT, so low upon earth,
    You send a flash to the sun.
    Here is the golden close of love,
    All my wooing is done.
Oh, the woods and the meadows,
    Woods where we hid from the wet,
Stiles where we stay'd to be kind,
    Meadows in which we met!
Light, so low in the vale
    You flash and lighten afar,
For this is the golden morning of love,
    And you are his morning star.
Flash, I am coming, I come,
    By meadow and stile and wood,
Oh, lighten into my eyes and my heart,
    Into my heart and my blood!
Heart, are you great enough
    For a love that never tires?
O heart, are you great enough for love?
    I have heard of thorns and briers.
Over the thorns and briers,
    Over the meadows and stiles,
Over the world to the end of it
    Flash for a million miles.

ALFRED LORD TENNYSON, 1809-1892

THE MARRIAGE CEREMONY

THE Vested Priest before the Altar stands :
Approach, come gladly, ye prepared, in sight
Of God and chosen friends, your troth to plight
With the symbolic ring, and willing hands
Solemnly joined. Now sanctify the bands
O Father ! – to the Espoused thy blessing give,
That mutually assisted they may live
Obedient, as here taught, to thy commands.
So prays the Church, to consecrate a Vow
"The which would endless matrimony make ;"
Union that shadows forth and doth partake
A mystery potent human love to endow
With heavenly, each more prized for the other's sake ;
Weep not, meek Bride ! uplift thy timid brow.

WILLIAM WORDSWORTH, 1770-1850

BRIDAL BALLAD

THE ring is on my hand,
    And the wreath is on my brow ;
Satins and jewels grand
Are all at my command,
    And I am happy now.

EDGAR ALLAN POE. 1809-1849

AN EPITHALAMION ON THE LADY
ELIZABETH

*W*HY virgin's girdle now untie,
   And in thy nuptial bed (love's altar) lie
    A pleasing sacrifice; now dispossess
Thee of these chains and robes which were put on
T'adorn the day, not thee; for thou, alone,
   Like virtue and truth, art best in nakedness;
   This bed is only to virginity
A grave, but, to a better state, a cradle;
Till now thou wast but able
   To be what now thou art; then that by thee
No more be said, *I may be*, but, *I am*,
Tonight put on perfection, and a woman's name.

JOHN DONNE, 1572-1631

ON MY WEDDING-DAY

*H*ERE's a happy new year! but with reason
I beg you'll permit me to say –
Wish me *many* returns of the *season*.
But as *few* as you please of the day.

January 2, 1820

LORD BYRON. 1788-1824

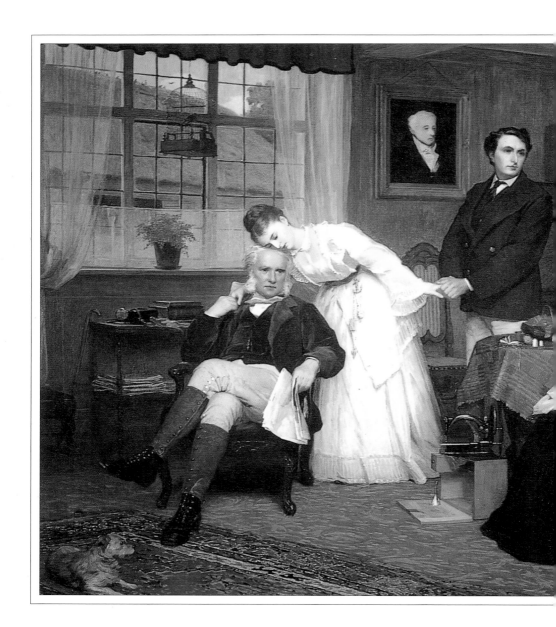

GOING AWAY

*S*OAMES, moving to the well of the staircase, saw June go, and drew a breath of satisfaction. Why didn't Fleur come? They would miss their train. That train would bear her away from him, yet he could not help fidgeting at the thought that they would lose it. And then she did come, running down in her tan-coloured frock and black velvet cap, and passed him into the drawing-room. He saw her kiss her mother, her aunt, Val's wife, Imogen, and then come forth, quick and pretty as ever. How would she treat him at this last moment of her girlhood? He couldn't hope for much!

Her lips pressed the middle of his cheek.

"Daddy!" she said, and was past and gone. Daddy! She hadn't called him that for years. He drew a long breath and followed slowly down. There was all the folly with that confetti stuff and the rest of it to go through with, yet. But he would like just to catch her smile, if she leaned out, though they would hit her in the eye with the shoe, if they didn't take care. Young Mont's voice said fervently in his ear:

"Good-bye, sir; and thank you! I'm so fearfully bucked."

"Good-bye," he said; "don't miss your train."

He stood on the bottom step but three, whence he could see above the heads – the silly hats and heads. They were in the car now; and there was that stuff, showering, and there went the shoe. A flood of something welled up in Soames, and – he didn't know – he couldn't see!

FROM *THE FORSYTE SAGA* BY JOHN GALSWORTHY, 1867-1933

SONG

*T*wo wedded lovers watched the rising moon,
   That with her strange mysterious beauty glowing,
   Over misty hills and waters flowing,
Crowned the long twilight loveliness of June :
    And thus in me, and thus in me, they spake,
    The solemn secret of first love did wake.

Above the hills the blushing orb arose ;
   Her shape encircled by a radiant bower,
   In which the nightingale with charmèd power
Poured forth enchantment o'er the dark repose :
    And thus in me, and thus in me, they said,
    Earth's mists did with the sweet new spirit wed.

Far up the sky with ever purer beam,
   Upon the throne of night the moon was seated,
   And down the valley glens the shades retreated,
And silver light was on the open stream.
    And thus in me, and thus in me, they sighed,
    Aspiring Love has hallowed Passion's tide.

GEORGE MEREDITH. 1828-1909

CHARITY ROYALL

AN HOUR later, coming out of the glare of the dining-room, she waited in the marble-panelled hall while Mr. Royall, before the brass lattice of one of the corner counters, selected a cigar and bought an evening paper. Men were lounging in rocking chairs under the blazing chandeliers, travellers coming and going, bells ringing, porters shuffling by with luggage....

Charity stood among these cross-currents of life as motionless and inert as if she had been one of the tables screwed to the marble floor. All her soul was gathered up into one sick sense of coming doom, and she watched Mr. Royall in fascinated terror while he pinched the cigars in successive boxes and unfolded his evening paper with a steady hand.

Presently he turned and joined her. " You go right along up to bed – I 'm going to sit down here and have my smoke," he said. He spoke as easily and naturally as if they had been an old couple, long used to each other's ways, and her contracted heart gave a flutter of relief.

FROM *SUMMER* BY EDITH WHARTON, 1862-1937

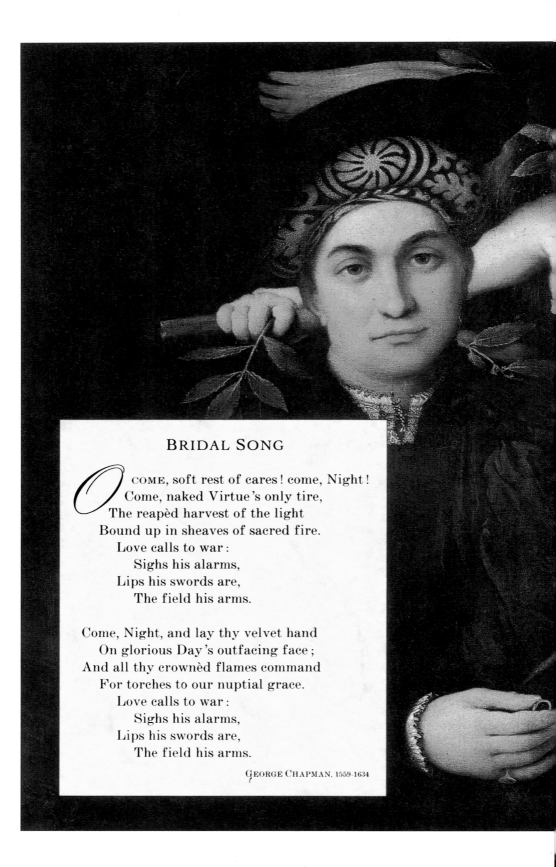

BRIDAL SONG

O COME, soft rest of cares! come, Night!
　Come, naked Virtue's only tire,
The reapèd harvest of the light
　Bound up in sheaves of sacred fire.
　　Love calls to war:
　　　Sighs his alarms,
　　Lips his swords are,
　　　The field his arms.

Come, Night, and lay thy velvet hand
　On glorious Day's outfacing face;
And all thy crownèd flames command
　For torches to our nuptial grace.
　　Love calls to war:
　　　Sighs his alarms,
　　Lips his swords are,
　　　The field his arms.

GEORGE CHAPMAN, 1559-1634

A Sense of Belonging

*P*ONSONBY had been a rather pretty, but pale and some-what peevish-looking girl; but Mrs. Crosbie was round and rosy and smiling, as if she had never known a care in the wide world.

"How well you are looking!" exclaimed Joan, as they met. "Why, I should hardly have known you again. Italy has worked miracles for you, Cecily. I have never seen you look so rosy before!"

"Oh, it isn't Italy," replied the bride, as she kissed unwilling Joan over and over again; "it's my Charlie, Miss Trevor. He's been so good to me, that my honeymoon has been a species of Paradise. I've been telling all the girls this afternoon to get married as soon as ever they can. They won't know what life is until they do!"

"But they might not get another Captain Crosbie," said Joan, laughing.

"No," replied Cecily, pursing her lips; "I suppose not; for I don't believe there can be two men like him in the world. But still they can get good men to love them; and what I mean is that they must not let a chance go by."

"I dare say you are right," said Joan, musingly, "and that mutual love is the best thing we can attain."

"Oh, it isn't only the love, dear!" replied Mrs. Crosbie, who seemed to have grown marvellously wise since they had parted. "Many people love, you know, and are very miserable in consequence; it's the beautiful security and freedom in marriage that makes it so happy. To feel that you actually *belong* to your husband – that you have a right to appeal to him for advice or assistance or protection whenever you require it; that all the world may know you love each other and you may glory in the fact – I think that is the grand thing that brings so much peace and pleasure with it!"

"But cannot one love in secret and feel just as happy?" questioned Joan. "Isn't there something more sacred in a private love that is not shared by the world?"

Mrs. Crosbie thought a moment and then shook her head.

FROM *A RATIONAL MARRIAGE* BY FLORENCE MARRYAT, 1838-1899

THE HAPPY HUSBAND

OFT, oft methinks, the while with Thee
    I breathe, as from the heart, thy dear
    And dedicated name, I hear
A promise and a mystery,
    A pledge of more than passing life,
    Yea, in that very name of Wife!

S.T. COLERIDGE, 1772-1834

MY WIFE

TRUSTY, dusky, vivid, true,
  With eyes of gold and bramble-dew,
  Steel-true and blade-straight,
The great artificer
Made my mate.

Honour, anger, valour, fire;
A love that life could never tire,
Death quench or evil stir,
The mighty master
Gave to her.

Teacher, tender, comrade, wife,
A fellow-farer true through life,
Heart-whole and soul-free
The august father
Gave to me.

ROBERT LOUIS STEVENSON, 1850-1894

A MATCH

*I*F LOVE were what the rose is,
    And I were like the leaf,
Our lives would grow together
In sad or singing weather,
Blown fields or flowerful closes,
    Green pleasure or grey grief;
If love were what the rose is,
    And I were like the leaf.

If I were what the words are,
    And love were like the tune,
With double sound and single
Delight our lips would mingle,
With kisses glad as birds are
    That get sweet rain at noon;
If I were what the words are,
    And love were like the tune.

If you were life, my darling,
    And I your love were death,
We'd shine and snow together
Ere March made sweet the weather
With daffodil and starling
    And hours of fruitful breath;
If you were life, my darling,
    And I your love were death.

ALGERNON CHARLES SWINBURNE. 1837-1909

THE GOOD MORROW

I WONDER BY my troth, what thou and I
    Did, till we loved? were we not weaned till then?
But sucked on country pleasures, childishly?
    Or snorted we i'the seven sleepers' den?
'Twas so; But this, all pleasures fancies be.
If ever any beauty I did see,
Which I desired, and got, 'twas but a dream of thee.

And now good morrow to our waking souls,
    Which watch not one another out of fear;
For love, all love of other sights controls,
    And makes one little room, an everywhere.
Let sea-discoverers to new worlds have gone,
Let maps to others, worlds on worlds have shown,
Let us possess our world, each hath one, and is one.

My face in thine eye, thine in mine appears,
    And true plain hearts do in the faces rest,
Where can we find two better hemispheres
    Without sharp North, without declining West?
Whatever dies, was not mixed equally;
If our two loves be one, or, thou and I
Love so alike, that none do slacken, none can die.

JOHN DONNE. 1572-1631

THE GRAND TOUR

THE QUEEN IN PARIS

St Cloud, 23rd August, 1855

I DO NOT intend to attempt any description, for I have no time for anything of the sort; besides I have no doubt you will read the papers, and I know good Van de Weyer has written *au long* to you about it all. I will therefore only give in a few words my impressions.

I am *delighted, enchanted, amused,* and *interested,* and think I never saw anything more *beautiful* and *gay* than Paris – or more splendid than all the Palaces. Our reception is *most* gratifying – for it is enthusiastic and really kind in the highest degree; and Maréchal Magnan (whom you know well) says that such a reception as I have received *every day here* is much greater and much more enthusiastic even than Napoleon on his return from his victories had received! Our entrance into Paris ... was quite *overpowering* – splendidly decorated – illuminated – immensely crowded – and 60,000 troops out – from the Gare de Strasbourg to St Cloud, of which 20,000 Gardes Nationales, who had come great distances to see me.

The Emperor has done wonders for Paris, and for the Bois de Boulogne. Everything is beautifully *monté* at Court – *very* quiet, and in excellent order; I must say we are both much struck with the difference between this and the poor King's time, when the noise, confusion, and bustle were great. We have been to the Exposition, to Versailles – which is most splendid and magnificent – to the Grand Opéra, where the reception and the way in which "God save the Queen" was sung were *most magnificent.* Yesterday we went to the Tuileries; in the evening *Théâtre ici*; to-night an immense ball at the Hôtel de Ville. They have asked to call a new street, which we opened, *after me*!

FROM *LETTERS OF QUEEN VICTORIA,* 1819-1901

LUNCH AT LAURENTS

T HE fresh spring sunshine which had so often attended Lizzie West on her dusty climb up the hill of St Cloud, beamed on her, some two years later in a scene and a situation of altered import.

Its rays, filtered through the horse chestnuts of the Champs Elysées, shone on the graveled circle about Laurent's restaurant; and Miss West, seated at a table within that privileged space, presented to the light a hat much better able to sustain its scrutiny than those which had shaded the brow of Juliet Deering's instructions.

Her dress was in keeping with the hat, and both belonged to a situation rife with such possibilities as the act of a leisurely luncheon at Laurent's in the opening week of the Salon. Her companions, of both sexes, confirmed this impression by an appropriateness of attire and an ease of manner implying the largest range of selection between the forms of Parisian idleness; and even Andora Macy, seated opposite, as in the place of co-hostess or companion, reflected, in coy greys and mauves, the festal note of the occasion.

FROM *THE LETTERS* BY EDITH WHARTON. 1862-1937

A VILLA ON THE RIVIERA

IT was at this villa in Cannes that the Rostoffs passed the winter – and it wasn't at all the thing to remind Princess Rostoff that this Riviera villa, from the marble fountain – after Bernini – to the gold cordial glasses – after dinner – was paid for with American gold.

The Russians, of course, were gay people on the Continent in the gala days before the war. Of the three races that used Southern France for a pleasure ground they were easily the most adept at the grand manner. The English were too practical, and the Americans, though they spent freely, had no tradition of romantic conduct. But the Russians – there was a people as gallant as the Latins, and rich besides! When the Rostoffs arrived at Cannes late in January the restaurateurs telegraphed north for the Prince's favorite labels to paste on their champagne, and the jewelers put incredibly gorgeous articles aside to show to him – but not to the princess – and the Russian Church was swept and garnished for the season that the Prince might beg orthodox forgiveness for his sins. Even the Mediterranean turned obligingly to a deep wine color in the spring evenings, and fishing boats with robin-breasted sails loitered exquisitely offshore.

In a vague way young Val realized that this was all for the benefit of him and his family. It was a privileged paradise, this white little city on the water, in which he was free to do what he liked because he was rich and young and the blood of Peter the Great ran indigo in his veins. He was only seventeen in 1914, when this history begins, but he had already fought a duel with a young man four years his senior, and he had a small hairless scar to show for it on top of his handsome head.

But the question of love in the night was the thing nearest his heart. It was a vague pleasant dream he had, something that was going to happen to him some day that would be unique and incomparable. He could have told no more about it than that there was a lovely unknown girl concerned in it, and that it ought to take place beneath the Riviera moon.

FROM *LOVE IN THE NIGHT* BY F. SCOTT FITZGERALD, 1896-1940

MARSEILLES

WE left this town towards evening, and took the road to
Marseilles. . . . I was there twice or thrice afterwards,
in fair weather and foul; and I am afraid there is no doubt
that it is a dirty and disagreeable place. But the prospect,
from the fortified heights, of the beautiful Mediterranean,
with its lovely rocks and islands, is most delightful. These
heights are a desirable retreat, for less picturesque reasons –
as an escape from a compound of vile smells perpetually
arising from a great harbour full of stagnant water, and
befouled by the refuse of innumerable ships with all sorts of
cargoes: which, in hot weather, is dreadful in the last degree.

There were foreign sailors, of all nations, in the streets;
with red shirts, blue shirts, buff shirts, tawny shirts, and
shirts of orange colour. . . . There were the townspeople sitting
in clusters on the pavement, or airing themselves on the tops
of their houses, or walking up and down the closest and least
airy of Boulevards; and there were crowds of fierce-looking
people of the lower sort, blocking up the way, constantly.

FROM *GOING THROUGH FRANCE* BY CHARLES DICKENS, 1812-1870

A MEDITERRANEAN
PROMONTORY

To look at it from the outside, the Cap d'Antibes is just a long low spit of dull olive-grey land, but, within, it has sea and mountain views most gloriously beautiful. To the east you see everything you can see from Nice, to the west you see everything you can see from Cannes; to the north, a gigantic range of snow-covered Alps; to the south, and all around, the sky-blue Mediterranean. For the Cape is a promontory made up of lots of little promontories, each jutting into the sea at all possible angles, and with endless miniature bays, mimic islets, their white rocks jagged and worn by the dashing waves, that break over them in ceaseless spray, even in glassy weather. To sit among oranges, olives, and palms, as at Algiers or Palermo, and yet look up from one's seat under one's vine and fig-tree, to see the snow-clad Alps glowing pink in the sunset as at Zermatt or Chamonix, is a combination of incongruous delights nowhere else to be met in Europe.

FROM *THE RIVIERAS* BY AUGUSTUS HARE, 1792-1834

THE STIMULATION OF
THE ALPS

To any one who should come from a southern sanatorium to the Alps, the row of sun-burned faces round the table would present the first surprise. He would begin by looking for the invalids, and he would lose his pains, for not one out of five of even the bad cases bears the mark of sickness on his face. The plump sunshine from above and its strong reverberation from below colour the skin like an Indian climate ; the treatment, which consists mainly of the open air, exposes even the sickliest to tan, and a tableful of invalids comes, in a month or two, to resemble a tableful of hunters. But although he may be thus surprised at the first glance, his astonishment will grow greater, as he experiences the effects of the climate on himself. In many ways it is a trying business to reside upon the Alps : the stomach is exercised, the appetite often languishes ; the liver may at times rebel ; and because you have come so far from metropolitan advantages, it does not follow that you shall recover. But one thing is undeniable – that in the rare air, clear, cold, and blinding light of Alpine winters, a man takes a certain troubled delight in his existence which can nowhere else be paralleled. He is perhaps no happier, but he is stingingly alive. It does not, perhaps, come out of him in work or exercise, yet he feels an enthusiasm of the blood unknown in more temperate climates. It may not be health, but it is fun.

FROM *ESSAYS OF TRAVEL* BY ROBERT LOUIS STEVENSON, 1850-1894

FLOATING VILLAGES

Let those who delight in picturesque country, repair to the borders of the Rhine, and follow the road which we took, from Bonn to Coblentz. In some places it is suspended like a cornice, above the waters; in others, it winds behind lofty steeps and broken acclivities, shaded by woods and cloathed with an endless variety of plants and flowers. Several green paths lead amongst this vegetation to the summits of the rocks, which often serve as the foundation of abbeys and castles, whose lofty roofs and spires, rising above the cliffs, impress passengers with ideas of their grandeur, that might probably vanish upon a nearer approach. Not chusing to lose any prejudice in their favour, I kept a respectful distance whenever I left my carriage, and walked on the banks of the river. Just before we came to Andernach, an antiquated town with strange morisco-looking towers, I spied a raft, at least three hundred feet in length, on which ten or twelve cottages were erected, and a great many people employed in sawing wood. The women sat spinning at their doors, whilst their children played among the water-lilies, that bloomed in abundance on the edge of the stream. A smoke, rising from one of these aquatic habitations, partially obscured the mountains beyond, and added not a little to their effect.

FROM *DREAMS, WAKING THOUGHTS, AND INCIDENTS*
BY WILLIAM BECKFORD, 1759-1844

WALKING THROUGH THE BLACK FOREST

FROM Baden-Baden we made the customary trip into the Black Forest. We were on foot most of the time. One cannot describe those noble woods, nor the feeling with which they inspire him. A feature of the feeling, however, is a deep sense of contentment; another feature of it is a buoyant, boyish gladness; and a third and very conspicuous feature of it is one's sense of the remoteness of the work-day world and his entire emancipation from it and its affairs.

Those woods stretch unbroken over a vast region; and everywhere they are such dense woods, and so still, and so piney and fragrant. The stems of the trees are trim and straight, and in many places all the ground is hidden for miles under a thick cushion of moss of a vivid green colour, with not a decayed or ragged spot in its surface, and not a fallen leaf or twig to mar its immaculate tidiness. A rich cathedral gloom pervades the pillared aisles; so the stray flecks of sunlight that strike a trunk here and a bough yonder are strongly accented, and when they strike the moss they fairly seem to burn. But the weirdest effect, and the most enchanting, is that produced by the diffused light of the low afternoon sun; no single ray is able to pierce its way in, then, but the diffused light takes colour from moss and foliage, and pervades the place like a faint, green-tinted mist, the theatrical fire of fairyland. The suggestion of mystery and the supernatural which haunts the forest at all times is intensified by this unearthly glow.

FROM *A TRAMP ABROAD* BY MARK TWAIN, 1835-1910

VIENNA

PERHAPS of all the great towns I ever was in Vienna is the very pleasantest, particularly at this time of the year. The number of people of fashion who reside here, the ease with which we were introduced, and the many places of public lounging, are beyond those of any town we have seen on the Continent. Bootle introduced us to some friends he had been acquainted with at Petersburg who happened to be here, and we presented our letters to Stratton, the chargé d'affaires. Such an introduction for an Englishman is quite sufficient, as the only question ever asked about you is, "Est-il aimable?" which I presume is the reason why Lord Porchester preferred Dresden, as there can otherwise be no comparison. A few evenings after our arrival we were carried to a great ball at a Madame de Saldaignac's; as she had assembled everything that was gay amongst the *haute noblesse* here, we began in a fair way. The dances in vogue here are the walses, and English country dances, so Heaven be praised we need not, as in France, torture our legs into cotillons, or have a dancing-master to teach us to hold up our heads. The walse, however, we have not yet dared to attempt. I showed Anne one day how it was danced, and if she has forgot Martignier can tell her; but in doing it the other day as part of a country dance I gave my partner such a kick that we were very near both falling together. They dance them so well here that I assure you it was a great subject of lamentation to us that we could not join in them ...

You here meet everybody, for the weather has been uncommonly fine, and people here dare amuse themselves, because it is not thought vulgar. In London it would be certainly thought rather odd, but in a broad, open street like St James's Street I have seen women of fashion, and even princesses with a hundred thousand quarterings, sitting eating ice at a coffee-house door after ten o'clock at night.

FROM *A GRAND TOUR* BY J. B. S. MORRITT, 1772-1843

ARRIVAL IN ITALY

Milan, April, 1818

BEHOLD us arrived at length at the end of our journey – that is, within a few miles of it – because we design to spend the summer on the shore of the Lake of Como. Our journey was somewhat painful from the cold – and in no other manner interesting until we passed the Alps: of course I except the Alps themselves; but no sooner had we arrived at Italy, than the loveliness of the earth and the serenity of the sky made the greatest difference in my sensations. I depend on these things for life; for in the smoke of cities, and the tumult of human kind, and the chilling fogs and rain of our own country, I can hardly be said to live. With what delight did I hear the woman, who conducted us to see the triumphal arch of Augustus at Susa, speak the clear and complete language of Italy, though half unintelligible to me, after that nasal and abbreviated cacophony of the French! A ruined arch of magnificent proportions in the Greek taste, standing in a kind of road of green lawn, overgrown with violets and primroses, and in the midst of stupendous mountains, and a *blonde* woman, of light and graceful manners, something in the style of Fuseli's Eve, were the first things we met in Italy.

FROM *LETTERS OF P. B. SHELLEY*, 1792-1822

BRIDGE OF SIGHS

I STOOD in Venice, on the Bridge of Sighs;
   A palace and a prison on each hand:
I saw from out the wave her structures rise
As from the stroke of the enchanter's wand:
A thousand years their cloudy wings expand
Around me, and a dying Glory smiles
O'er the far times, when many a subject land
Look'd to the winged Lion's marble piles,
Where Venice sate in state, throned on her hundred isles!

FROM *CHILDE HAROLD'S PILGRIMAGE* BY LORD BYRON, 1788-1824

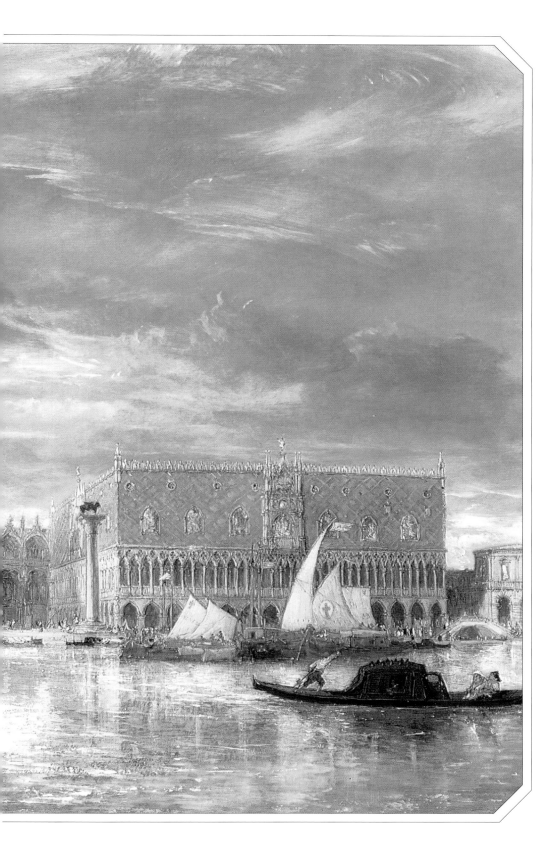

A ROOM WITH A VIEW

It was pleasant to wake up in Florence, to open the eyes upon a bright bare room, with a floor of red tiles which look clean though they are not; with a painted ceiling whereon pink griffins and blue amorini sport in a forest of yellow violins and bassoons. It was pleasant, too, to fling wide the windows, pinching the fingers in unfamiliar fastenings, to lean out into sunshine with beautiful hills and trees and marble churches opposite, and, close below, the Arno, gurgling against the embankment of the road.

Over the river men were at work with spades and sieves on the sandy foreshore, and on the river was a boat, also diligently employed for some mysterious end. An electric tram came rushing underneath the window. No one was inside it, except one tourist; but its platforms were overflowing with Italians, who preferred to stand. Children tried to hang on behind, and the conductor, with no malice, spat in their faces to make them let go. Then soldiers appeared – good-looking, undersized men – wearing each a knapsack covered with mangy fur, and a greatcoat which had been cut for some larger soldier. Beside them walked officers, looking foolish and fierce, and before them went little boys, turning somersaults in time with the band. The tram-car became entangled in their ranks, and moved on painfully, like a caterpillar in a swarm of ants. One of the little boys fell down, and some white bullocks came out of an archway. Indeed, if it had not been for the good advice of an old man who was selling buttonhooks, the road might never have got clear.

Over such trivialities as these many a valuable hour may slip away, and the traveller who has gone to Italy to study the tactile values of Giotto, or the corruption of the Papacy, may return remembering nothing but the blue sky and the men and women who live under it.

FROM *A ROOM WITH A VIEW* BY E. M. FORSTER. 1879-1970

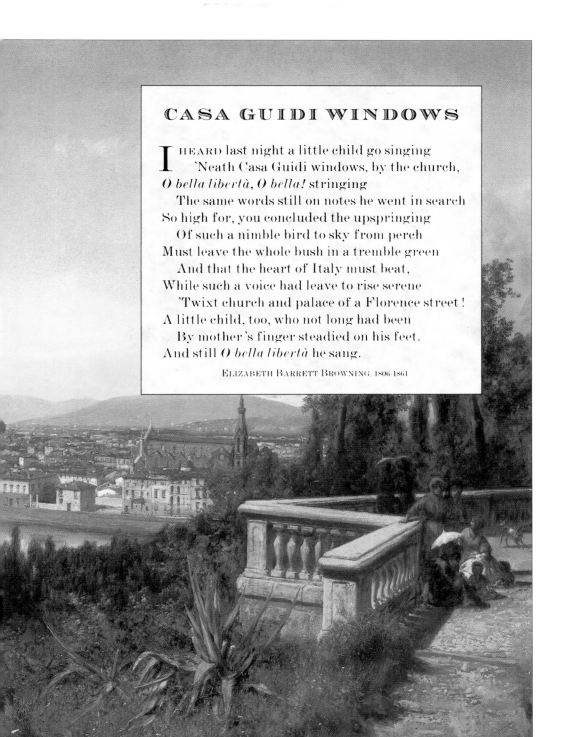

CASA GUIDI WINDOWS

I HEARD last night a little child go singing
    'Neath Casa Guidi windows, by the church,
O bella libertà, O bella! stringing
    The same words still on notes he went in search
So high for, you concluded the upspringing
    Of such a nimble bird to sky from perch
Must leave the whole bush in a tremble green
    And that the heart of Italy must beat,
While such a voice had leave to rise serene
    'Twixt church and palace of a Florence street!
A little child, too, who not long had been
    By mother's finger steadied on his feet.
And still *O bella libertà* he sang.

ELIZABETH BARRETT BROWNING, 1806-1861

FIRST IMPRESSIONS OF ROME

I MAY not attempt to report in its fulness our young woman's response to the deep appeal of Rome, to analyse her feelings as she trod the pavement of the Forum or to number her pulsations as she crossed the threshold of Saint Peter's. It is enough to say that her impression was such as might have been expected of a person of her freshness and her eagerness. She had always been fond of history, and here was history in the stones of the street and the atoms of the sunshine. She had an imagination that kindled at the mention of great deeds, and wherever she turned some great deed had been acted. These things strongly moved her, but moved her all inwardly. It seemed to her companions that she talked less than usual, and Ralph Touchett, when he appeared to be looking listlessly and awkwardly over her head, was really dropping on her an intensity of observation. By her own measure she was very happy; she would even have been willing to take these hours for the happiest she was ever to know. The sense of the terrible human past was heavy to her, but that of something altogether contemporary would suddenly give it wings that it could wave in the blue.

FROM *THE PORTRAIT OF A LADY* BY HENRY JAMES, 1843-1916

GROTTO AZZURRO, CAPRI

TO-DAY we visited Capri.... In two hours we reached the island, and ran into the little bay in which the town of Capri is situated. We then transferred ourselves to two small boats, for the purpose of visiting the Grotto Azzurro. We were rowed under the high, dark, bare, perpendicular cliffs, and with anxious curiosity I looked for the opening to the grotto. The mountains grew higher, the precipices more abrupt and black, as we rowed slowly in the deep calm water beneath their shadow. At length we came to a small opening; it was necessary to sit at the bottom of the boat, as it shot through the narrow, low, covered entrance; within, the strangest sight is revealed: we entered a large cavern, formed by the sea; the hue resembles that which I mentioned as belonging to the caves of the Sorrentine coast; only here it is brighter – a turquoise, milky, pellucid, living azure. The white roof and walls of the cave reflect the tints, and the shimmering motion of the waves being also mirrored on the rock, the effect is more fairy-like and strange than can be conceived. This cave was discovered by two Englishmen, who went to swim under the cliffs, and penetrated by chance its narrow opening. It deserves the renown it has gained. I cannot explain from what effect of the laws of light this singular and beautiful hue proceeds. Partly it is the natural azure of the waves of this bright sea, which, entering, reflects the snow-white cavern, and is turned as it were into transparent milk; another cause may be, that the walls of the cavern do not reach deeper than the surface of the water; they just touch it – and the sea flows beneath. The water is icy cold, and the adventure would be perilous; but a good swimmer might be excited to dive beneath the paving water, strike out under the cave, and seek for wonders beyond.

FROM *RAMBLES IN GERMANY AND ITALY* BY MARY SHELLEY. 1797-1851

A GREEK WELCOME

I<small>N</small> their intercourse with strangers the Greeks are friendly, civil, and, as a rule, not officious or importunate, though the male inhabitants of a village, old and young, may sometimes show their curiosity by clustering round the traveller. Offers of service, such as are common in Italy, are rare. The tourist therefore pursues his way without molestation, though, when his time is limited, he may miss the sharp little Italian ragazzi, who seem to divine the stranger's intentions by instinct and conduct him to the wished for spots for a fee of a few soldi. The inordinate idea of the importance of travellers that prevails in S. Italy is also found in Greece ; and the lower classes cherish a firm conviction that every foreigner (λορδος, "lord") is enormously rich.

KARL BAEDEKER, 1801-1859

ESSENTIAL PACKING

T HE traveller is strongly recommended to take with him a supply of curry-powder, a bottle of Worcestershire sauce, and a few pots of marmalade. These three items will often make all the difference between an eatable and an uneatable meal. Butter is unknown (except for cooking purposes) in the provinces of Greece, and even in Athens the substance served under that name at table much more nearly resembles an inferior kind of Devonshire cream.

FROM *MURRAY'S HANDBOOK FOR TRAVELLERS IN GREECE* BY JOHN MURRAY, 1745-1793

HOME THOUGHTS
FROM ABROAD

O TO be in England
Now that April's there,
And whoever wakes in England
Sees, some morning, unaware,
That the lowest boughs and the brushwood sheaf
Round the elm-tree bole are in tiny leaf,
While the chaffinch sings on the orchard bough
In England – now!

ROBERT BROWNING, 1812-1889

MOTHER *and* CHILD

Awaiting the Birth

A LESS dismal preoccupation came to distract him – his wife's pregnancy. The nearer her time drew, the fonder husband he became. It made a new bond of the flesh between them, a constant reminder of their growing union. When he watched from a distance her indolent gait, her body turning limply on her uncorseted hips, when he feasted his eyes on her as she lounged wearily in her easy chair opposite him, his happiness overflowed: he went over and kissed her, stroked her cheek, called her "little mummy", tried to dance her round the room, and uttered between tears and laughter all manner of playful endearments that came into his head. He was overjoyed at the idea of becoming a father. Nothing was lacking to him now. He had been through the whole of human experience: serenely he settled down with both elbows firmly planted upon the table of life.

After her first feeling of astonishment Emma was eager to have the child and so find out what it felt like to be a mother.

She wanted a son. He should be dark and strong, and she would call him Georges. The thought of having a male child afforded her a kind of anticipatory revenge for all her past helplessness. A man, at any rate, is free. He can explore the passions and the continents, can surmount obstacles, reach out to the most distant joys. Whereas a woman is constantly thwarted. At once inert and pliant, she has to contend with both physical weakness and legal subordination. Her will is like the veil on her bonnet, fastened by a single string and quivering at every breeze that blows. Always there is a desire that impels and a convention that restrains.

The baby was born at about six o'clock one Sunday morning as the sun was rising.

"It's a girl," said Charles.

She turned away and fainted.

FROM *MADAME BOVARY* BY GUSTAVE FLAUBERT, 1821-1880

THE ANGELS ARE STOOPING

THE angels are stooping
  Above your bed ;
They weary of trooping
With the whimpering dead.

God's laughing in Heaven
To see you so good ;
The Sailing Seven
Are gay with His mood.

I sigh that kiss you,
For I must own
That I shall miss you
When you have grown.

W B YEATS. 1865-1939

THE BABY'S DANCE

DANCE, little baby, dance up high,
　Never mind baby, mother is by ;
Crow and caper, caper and crow,
There little baby, there you go :
Up to the ceiling, down to the ground,
Backwards and forwards, round and round.
Then dance, little baby, and mother shall sing,
With the merry gay coral, ding, ding, a-ding, ding.

ANN TAYLOR. 1782-1866

A CRADLE SONG

SWEET dreams form a shade,
O 'er my lovely infants head.
Sweet dreams of pleasant streams.
By happy silent moony beams.

Sweet sleep with soft down,
Weave thy brows an infant crown.
Sweet sleep Angel mild,
Hover o 'er my happy child.

Sweet smiles in the night,
Hover over my delight.
Sweet smiles Mothers smiles
All the livelong night beguiles.

Sweet moans, dovelike sighs,
Chase not slumber from thy eyes.
Sweet moans, sweeter smiles.
All the dovelike moans beguiles.

Sleep sleep happy child.
All creation slept and smil 'd.
Sleep sleep, happy sleep.
While o 'er thee thy mother weep.

WILLIAM BLAKE. 1757-1827

INTIMATIONS OF IMMORTALITY

FROM RECOLLECTIONS OF EARLY CHILDHOOD

OUR birth is but a sleep and a forgetting :
The Soul that rises with us, our life's Star,
Hath had elsewhere its setting,
And cometh from afar :
Not in entire forgetfulness,
And not in utter nakedness,
But trailing clouds of glory do we come
From God, who is our home :
Heaven lies about us in our infancy !
Shades of the prison-house begin to close
Upon the growing Boy,
But He beholds the light, and whence it flows,
He sees it in his joy ;
The Youth, who daily farther from the east
Must travel, still is Nature's Priest,
And by the vision splendid
Is on his way attended ;
At length the Man perceives it die away,
And fade into the light of common day.

WILLIAM WORDSWORTH, 1770-1850

MOTHERHOOD

Natásha had married in the early spring of 1813, and in 1820 already had three daughters, besides a son for whom she had longed and whom she was now nursing. She had grown stouter and broader, so that it was difficult to recognize the slim lively Natásha of former days in this robust motherly woman. Her features were more defined and had a calm, soft and serene expression. In her face there was none of the ever-glowing animation that had formerly burned there and constituted its charm. Now her face and body were often all that one saw, and her soul was not visible at all. All that struck the eye was a strong, handsome and fertile woman. The old fire very rarely kindled in her face now. That happened only when, as was the case that day, her husband returned home, or a sick child was convalescent, or on the rare occasions when something happened to induce her to sing, a practice she had quite abandoned since her marriage. At the rare moments when the old fire kindled in her handsome fully-developed body she was even more attractive than in former days.

All who had known Natásha before her marriage wondered at the change in her as at something extraordinary. Only the old countess, with her maternal instinct, had realized that all Natásha's outbursts had been due to her need of children and a husband and her mother was now surprised by the surprise expressed by those who had never understood Natásha, and kept saying that she had always known that Natásha would make an exemplary wife and mother.

"Only she lets her love of her husband and children overflow all bounds," said the countess, "so that it even becomes absurd."

From War and Peace by Count Leo Tolstoy, 1828-1910

MATERNAL DEVOTION

"Give him to me – give him to me," said the young mother. "Give him to me, Mary," and she almost tore the child out of her sister's arms. The poor little fellow murmured somewhat at the disturbance, but nevertheless nestled himself close into his mother's bosom.

"Here, Mary, take the cloak from me. My own, own darling, darling, darling jewel. You are not false to me. Everybody else is false; everybody else is cruel. Mamma will care for nobody, nobody, nobody, but her own, own, own little man;" and she again kissed and pressed the baby, and cried till the tears ran down over the child's face.

"He is a darling – as true as gold. What would mamma do without him? Mamma would lie down and die if she had not her own Johnny Bold to give her comfort." This and much more she said of the same kind, and for a time made no other answer to Mary's inquiries.

This kind of consolation from the world's deceit is very common.

Mothers obtain it from their children, and men from their dogs. Some men even do so from their walking sticks, which is just as rational. How is it that we can take joy to ourselves in that we are not deceived by those who have not attained the art to deceive us? In a true man, if such can be found, or a true woman, much consolation may indeed be taken.

In the caresses of her child, however, Eleanor did receive consolation; and may ill befall the man who would begrudge it to her.

From *Barchester Towers* by Anthony Trollope. 1815-1882

To an Infant

Ah, cease thy Tears and Sobs, my little Life!
I did but snatch away the unclasped Knife:
Some safer Toy will soon arrest thine eye
And to quick Laughter change this peevish cry!
Poor Stumbler on the rocky coast of Woe,
Tutored by Pain each source of Pain to know
Alike the foodful fruit and scorching fire
Awake thy eager grasp and young desire:
Alike the Good, the Ill offend thy sight,
And rouse the stormy Sense of shrill Affright!
Untaught, yet wise! mid all thy brief alarms
Thou closely clingest to thy Mother's arms,
Nestling thy little face in that fond breast
Whose anxious Heavings lull thee to thy rest!

Man's breathing Miniature! thou mak'st me sigh –
A Babe art thou – and such a Thing am I!
To anger rapid and as soon appeased,
For trifles mourning and by trifles pleased,
Break Friendship's Mirror with a tetchy blow,
Yet snatch what coals of fire on Pleasure's altar glow!

SAMUEL TAYLOR COLERIDGE. 1772-1831

Choosing a Name

I HAVE got a new-born sister;
   I was nigh the first that kissed her.
When the nursing woman brought her
To papa, his infant daughter,
How papa's dear eyes did glisten! –
She will shortly be to christen:
And papa has made the offer,
I shall have the naming of her.

Now I wonder what would please her,
Charlotte, Julia, or Louisa.
Ann and Mary, they 're too common;
Joan 's too formal for a woman;
Jane 's a prettier name beside;
But we had a Jane that died.
They would say, if 'twas Rebecca,
That she was a little Quaker.
Edith 's pretty, but that looks
Better in old English books;
Ellen 's left off long ago;
Blanche is out of fashion now.
None that I have named as yet
Are so good as Margaret.
Emily is neat and fine.
What do you think of Caroline?
How I 'm puzzled and perplexed
What to choose or think of next!
I am in a little fever.
Lest the name that I shall give her
Should disgrace her or defame her,
I will leave papa to name her.

CHARLES AND MARY LAMB, 1775-1834 & 1764-1847

—134—

To a Child

Dancing in the Wind

D<small>ANCE</small> there upon the shore;
 What need have you to care
For wind or water's roar?
And tumble out your hair
That the salt drops have wet;
Being young you have not known
The fool's triumph, nor yet
Love lost as soon as won,
Nor the best labourer dead
And all the sheaves to bind.
What need have you to dread
The monstrous crying of wind?

W B Y<small>EATS</small>, 1865-1939

If No One Ever Marries Me

If no one ever marries me –
   And I don't see why they should,
For nurse says I'm not pretty
   And I'm seldom very good –

If no one ever marries me
   I shan't mind very much ;
I shall buy a squirrel in a cage,
   And a little rabbit hutch.

I shall have a cottage near a wood,
   And a pony all my own,
And a little lamb, quite clean and tame,
   That I can take to town.

And when I'm getting really old,
   At twenty eight or nine,
I shall buy a little orphan girl
   And bring her up as mine.

LAURENCE ALMA-TADEMA. C. 1865-1940

VESPERS

Little Boy kneels at the foot of the bed,
Droops on the little hands little gold head.
Hush! Hush! Whisper who dares!
Christopher Robin is saying his prayers.

God bless Mummy. I know that's right.
Wasn't it fun in the bath tonight?
The cold's so cold, and the hot's so hot.
Oh! *God bless Daddy* – I quite forgot.

If I open my fingers a little bit more,
I can see Nanny's dressing-gown on the door.
It's a beautiful blue, but it hasn't a hood.
Oh! *God bless Nanny and make her good.*

Mine has a hood, and I lie in bed,
And pull the hood right over my head,
And I shut my eyes, and I curl up small,
And nobody knows that I'm there at all.

Oh! *Thank you, God, for a lovely day.*
And what was the other I had to say?
I said "Bless Daddy," so what can it be?
Oh, Now I remember it. *God bless Me.*

A A MILNE, 1882-1956

THE TIDE RIVER

CLEAR and cool, clear and cool,
  By laughing shallow, and dreaming pool ;
Cool and clear, cool and clear,
  By shining shingle, and foaming weir ;
Under the crag where the ouzel sings,
And the ivied wall where the church-bell rings,
    Undefiled, for the undefiled ;
  Play by me, bathe in me, mother and child.

  Dank and foul, dank and foul,
By the smoky town in its murky cowl ;
  Foul and dank, foul and dank,
By wharf and sewer and slimy bank ;
Darker and darker the further I go,
Baser and baser the richer I grow ;
    Who dare sport with the sin-defiled ?
  Shrink from me, turn from me, mother and child.

CHARLES KINGSLEY, 1819-1875

How to Write a Letter

MARIA intended a letter to write,
But could not begin (as she thought) to indite;
So went to her mother with pencil and slate,
Containing "Dear Sister", and also a date.

"With nothing to say, my dear girl, do not think
Of wasting your time over paper and ink;
But certainly this is an excellent way,
To try with your slate to find something to say.

"I will give you a rule," said her mother, "my dear,
Just think for a moment your sister is here,
And what would you tell her? Consider, and then,
Though silent your tongue, you can speak with your pen."

ELIZABETH TURNER. 1775 ?-1846

A LESSON FOR MAMMA

DEAR Mamma, if you just could be
  A tiny little girl like me,
And I your mamma, you would see
    How nice I'd be to you.
I'd always let you have your way ;
I'd never frown at you and say,
    " You are behaving ill today,
    Such conduct will not do. "

I'd always give you jelly-cake
For breakfast, and I'd never shake
My head, and say, " You must not take
    So very large a slice. "
I'd never say, " My dear, I trust
You will not make me say you *must*
Eat up your oatmeal " ; or " The crust
    You'll find, is very nice. "

I'd never say, " Well, just a *few* ! "
I'd let you stop your lessons too ;
I'd say, " They are too hard for you,
    Poor child, to understand. "
I'd put the books and slates away ;
You shouldn't do a thing but play,
And have a party every day.
    Ah-h-h ! wouldn't that be grand !

SYDNEY DAYRE (MRS COCHRAN) FL. 1881

IF . . .

IF you can keep your head when all about you
   Are losing theirs and blaming it on you,
If you can trust yourself when all men doubt you,
   But make allowance for their doubting too ;
If you can wait and not be tired by waiting,
   Or being lied about, don't deal in lies,
Or being hated, don't give way to hating,
   And yet don't look too good, nor walk too wise :

If you can dream – and not make dreams your master ;
   If you can think – and not make thoughts your aim ;
If you can meet with Triumph and Disaster
   And treat those two impostors just the same ;
If you can bear to hear the truth you've spoken
   Twisted by knaves to make a trap for fools,
Or watch the things you gave your life to, broken,
   And stoop and build 'em up with worn-out tools :

If you can talk with crowds and keep your virtue,
   Or walk with Kings – nor lose the common touch,
If neither foes nor loving friends can hurt you,
   If all men count with you, but none too much ;
If you can fill the unforgiving minute
   With sixty seconds' worth of distance run,
Yours is the Earth and everything that's in it,
   And – which is more – you'll be a Man, my son !

RUDYARD KIPLING, 1865-1936

THOUGHTS OF MARRIAGE

LADY C. Marry, that " marry " is the very theme
I came to talk of. Tell me, daughter Juliet,
How stands your dispositions to be married?
JUL. It is an honour that I dream not of.
NURSE. An honour! Were not I thine only nurse,
I would say thou hadst suck'd wisdom from thy teat.
LADY C. Well, think of marriage now.
Younger than you,
Here in Verona, ladies of esteem,
Are made already mothers. By my count,
I was your mother much upon these years
That you are now a maid. Thus, then, in brief :
The valiant Paris seeks you for his love.
NURSE. A man, young lady! lady, such a man
As all the world – why, he's a man of wax.
LADY C. Verona's summer hath not such a flower.
NURSE. Nay, he's a flower; in faith, a very flower.
LADY C. What say you? Can you love the gentleman?
This night you shall behold him at our feast ;
Read o'er the volume of young Paris' face,
And find delight writ there with beauty's pen ;
Examine every married lineament,
And see how one another lends content ;
And what obscur'd in this fair volume lies
Find written in the margent of his eyes.
This precious book of love, this unbound lover,
To beautify him, only lacks a cover.
This fish lives in the sea, and 'tis much pride
For fair without the fair within to hide.
That book in many's eyes doth share the glory
That in gold clasps locks in the golden story ;
So shall you share all that he doth possess,
By having him making yourself no less.
NURSE. No less! Nay, bigger ; women grow by men.
LADY C. Speak briefly, can you like of Paris' love?
JUL. I'll look to like, if looking liking move ;
But no more deep will I endart mine eye
Than your consent gives strength to make it fly.

FROM *ROMEO AND JULIET* BY WILLIAM SHAKESPEARE, 1564-1616

MY BOY JACK

"H AVE you news of my boy Jack?"
　　Not this tide.
"When d'you think that he'll come back?"
　　Not with this wind blowing, and this tide.

"Has any one else had word of him?"
　　Not this tide.
For what is sunk will hardly swim,
　　Not with this wind blowing, and this tide.

"Oh, dear, what comfort can I find!"
　　None this tide,
　　Nor any tide,
Except he did not shame his kind —
　　Not even with that wind blowing, and that tide.

Then hold your head up all the more,
　　This tide,
　　And every tide;
Because he was the son you bore,
　　And gave to that wind blowing and that tide!

RUDYARD KIPLING, 1865-1936

MOTHER O' MINE

(DEDICATION TO "THE LIGHT THAT FAILED")

IF I were hanged on the highest hill,
   Mother o' mine, O mother o' mine!
I know whose love would follow me still,
Mother o' mine, O mother o' mine!

If I were drowned in the deepest sea,
Mother o' mine, O mother o' mine!
I know whose tears would come down to me,
Mother o' mine, O mother o' mine!

If I were damned of body and soul,
I know whose prayer would make me whole,
Mother o' mine, O mother o' mine!

RUDYARD KIPLING, 1865-1936

CHRISTMAS

⇥❙HAPPY, HAPPY CHRISTMAS❙⇤

CHRISTMAS time! That man must be a misanthrope indeed, in whose breast something like a jovial feeling is not roused–in whose mind some pleasant associations are not awakened–by the recurrence of Christmas. There are people who will tell you that Christmas is not to them what it used to be; that each succeeding Christmas has found some cherished hope, or happy prospect, of the year before, dimmed or passed away; that the present only serves to remind them of reduced circumstances and straitened incomes – of the feasts they once bestowed on hollow friends, and of the cold looks that meet them now, in adversity and misfortune. Never heed such dismal reminiscences. There are few men who have lived long enough in the world, who cannot call up such thoughts any day in the year. Then do not select the merriest of the three hundred and sixty-five for your doleful recollections, but draw your chair nearer the blazing fire–fill the glass and send round the song—and if your room be smaller than it was a dozen years ago, or if your glass be filled with reeking punch, instead of sparkling wine, put a good face on the matter, and empty it off-hand, and fill another, and troll off the old ditty you used to sing, and thank God it's no worse . . .

Who can be insensible to the outpourings of good feeling, and the honest interchange of affectionate attachment which abound at this season of the year. A Christmas family-party! We know nothing in nature more delightful! There seems a magic in the very name of Christmas. Petty jealousies and discords are forgotten; social feelings are awakened, in bosoms to which they have long been strangers; father and son, or brother and sister, who have met and passed with averted gaze, or a look of cold recognition, for months before, proffer and return the cordial embrace, and bury their past animosities in their present happiness. Kindly hearts that have yearned towards each other but have been withheld by false notions of pride and self-dignity, are again reunited, and all is kindness and benevolence! Would that Christmas lasted the whole year through (as it ought) and that the prejudices and passions which deform our better nature were never called into action among those to whom they should ever be strangers!

FROM *SKETCHES BY BOZ* BY CHARLES DICKENS, 1812–1870

❧ CHRISTMAS WAS COMING ❧

GRADUALLY there gathered the feeling of expectation. Christmas was coming. In the shed, at nights, a secret candle was burning, a sound of veiled voices was heard. The boys were learning the old mystery play of St. George and Beelzebub. Twice a week, by lamplight, there was choir practice in the church, for the learning of old carols Brangwen wanted to hear. The girls went to these practices. Everywhere was a sense of mystery and rousedness. Everybody was preparing for something.

The time came near, the girls were decorating the church, with cold fingers binding holly and fir and yew about the pillars, till a new spirit was in the church, the stone broke out into dark, rich leaf, the arches put forth their æuds, and cold flowers rose to blossom in the dim, mystic atmosphere. Ursula must weave mistletoe over the door, and over the screen, and hang a silver dove from a sprig of yew, till dusk came down, and the church was like a grove.

In the cow-shed the boys were blacking their faces for a dress-rehearsal; the turkey hung dead, with opened, speckled wings, in the dairy. The time was come to make pies, in readiness.

The expectation grew more tense. The star was risen into the sky, the songs, the carols were ready to hail it. The star was the sign in the sky. Earth too should give a sign. As evening drew on, hearts beat fast with anticipation, hands were full of ready gifts. There were the tremulously expectant words of the church service, the night was past and the morning was come, the gifts were given and received, joy and peace made a flapping of wings in each heart, there was a great burst of carols, the Peace of the World had dawned, strife had passed away, every hand was linked in hand, every heart was singing.

FROM *THE RAINBOW* BY D. H. LAWRENCE, 1885-1930

GOOD CHRISTIAN MEN, REJOICE

Good Christian men, rejoice
　　With heart and soul and voice!
　　Now ye hear of endless bliss:
Joy! Joy!
　Jesus Christ was born for this.
He hath oped the heavenly door,
And man is blest for evermore.
　　Christ was born for this.

JOHN MASON NEALE, 1818–1866

ᐸᢒᔈ WINTER ᔈᢒᐳ

A WRINKLED, crabbed man they picture thee,
  Old Winter, with a rugged beard as grey
 As the long moss upon the apple-tree;
Blue lipt, an ice-drop at thy sharp blue nose;
  Close muffled up, and on thy dreary way,
Plodding alone through sleet and drifting snows.

They should have drawn thee by the high-heapt hearth,
  Old Winter! seated in thy great armed chair,
Watching the children at their Christmas mirth,
  Or circled by them, as thy lips declare
Some merry jest, or tale of murder dire,
  Or troubled spirit that disturbs the night,
Pausing at times to rouse the mouldering fire,
  Or taste the old October brown and bright.

ROBERT SOUTHEY, 1774–1843

ℰ. CHRISTMAS ℰ

THE bells of waiting Advent ring,
    The Tortoise stove is lit again
And lamp-oil light across the night
    Has caught the streaks of winter rain
In many a stained-glass window sheen
From Crimson Lake to Hooker's Green.

The holly in the windy hedge
    And round the Manor House the yew
Will soon be stripped to deck the ledge,
    The altar, font and arch and pew,
So that the villagers can say
"The church looks nice" on Christmas Day.

Provincial public houses blaze
    And Corporation tramcars clang,
On lighted tenements I gaze
    Where paper decorations hang,
And bunting in the red Town Hall
Says "Merry Christmas to you all"

And London shops on Christmas Eve
    Are strung with silver bells and flowers
As hurrying clerks the City leave
    To pigeon-haunted classic towers,
And marbled clouds go scudding by
The many-steepled London sky.

And girls in slacks remember Dad,
    And oafish louts remember Mum,
And sleepless children's hearts are glad,
    And Christmas-morning bells say "Come!"
Even to shining ones who dwell
Safe in the Dorchester Hotel.

And is it true? And is it true,
    This most tremendous tale of all,
Seen in a stained-glass window's hue,
    A Baby in an ox's stall?
The Maker of the stars and sea
Become a Child on earth for me?

And is it true? For if it is,
    No loving fingers tying strings
Around those tissued fripperies,
    The sweet and silly Christmas things,
Bath salts and inexpensive scent
And hideous tie so kindly meant,

No love that in a family dwells,
    No carolling in frosty air,
Nor all the steeple-shaking bells
    Can with this single Truth compare-
That God was Man in Palestine
And lives to-day in Bread and Wine.

JOHN BETJEMAN, 1906-1984

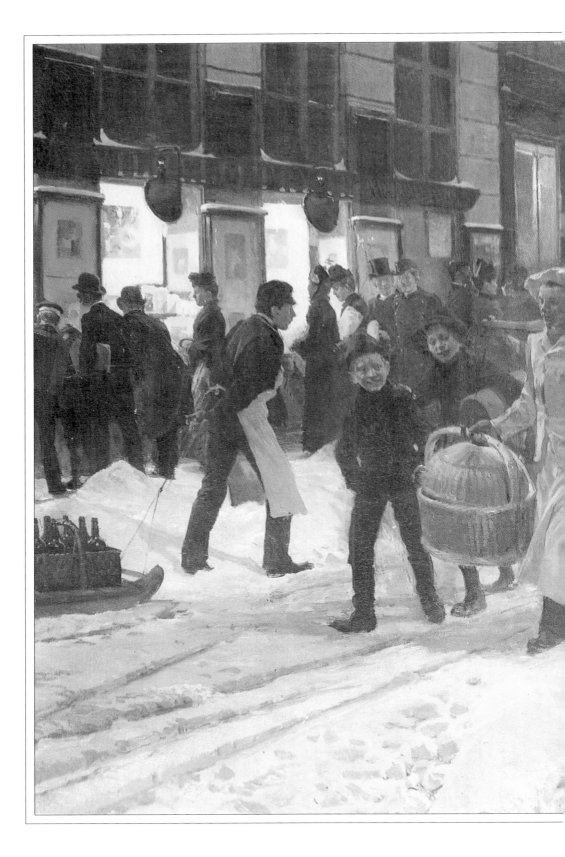

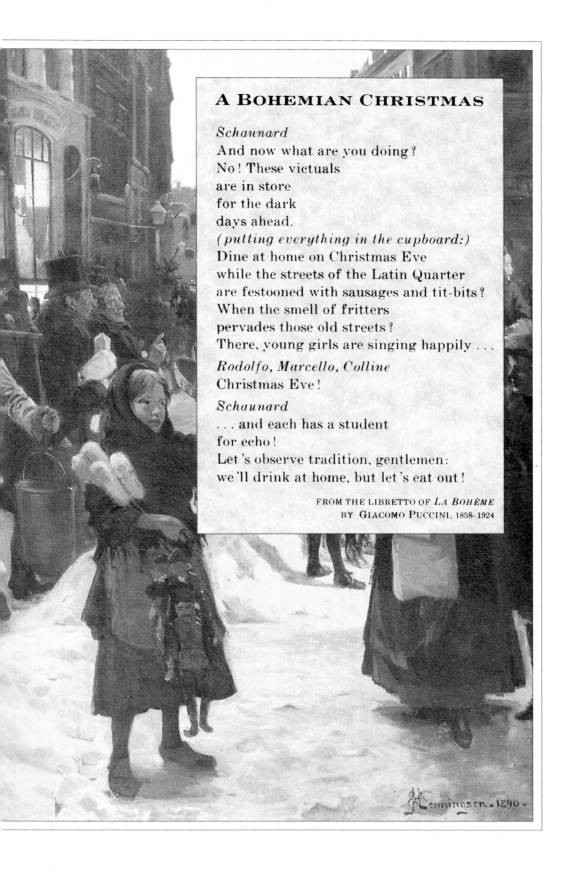

A BOHEMIAN CHRISTMAS

Schaunard
And now what are you doing?
No! These victuals
are in store
for the dark
days ahead.
(putting everything in the cupboard:)
Dine at home on Christmas Eve
while the streets of the Latin Quarter
are festooned with sausages and tit-bits?
When the smell of fritters
pervades those old streets?
There, young girls are singing happily ...

Rodolfo, Marcello, Colline
Christmas Eve!

Schaunard
... and each has a student
for echo!
Let's observe tradition, gentlemen:
we'll drink at home, but let's eat out!

FROM THE LIBRETTO OF *LA BOHÈME*
BY GIACOMO PUCCINI, 1858–1924

᜵᜶. AND IT CAME TO PASS ᜶᜵

ᴀɴᴅ Joseph also went up from Galilee, out of the city of Nazareth, into Judæa, unto the city of David, which is called Bethlehem; (because he was of the house and lineage of David:)

To be taxed with Mary his espoused wife, being great with child.

And so it was, that, while they were there, the days were accomplished that she should be delivered.

And she brought forth her first-born son, and wrapped him in swaddling clothes, and laid him in a manger; because there was no room for them in the inn.

And there were in the same country shepherds abiding in the field, keeping watch over their flock by night.

And, lo, the angel of the Lord came upon them, and the glory of the Lord shone round about them: and they were sore afraid.

And the angel said unto them, Fear not: for, behold, I bring you good tidings of great joy, which shall be to all people.

For unto you is born this day in the city of David a Saviour, which is Christ the Lord.

THE GOSPEL ACCORDING TO ST. LUKE, 2

❧ A CHRISTMAS CAROL ❧

THE Christ-child lay on Mary's lap,
　　His hair was like a light,
(O weary, weary were the world,
　　But here is all aright.)

The Christ-child lay on Mary's breast,
　　His hair was like a star.
(O stern and cunning are the kings,
　　But here the true hearts are.)

The Christ-child lay on Mary's heart,
　　His hair was like a fire.
(O weary, weary is the world,
　　But here the world's desire.)

The Christ-child stood at Mary's knee,
　　His hair was like a crown,
And all the flowers looked up at him,
　　And all the stars looked down.

G. K. CHESTERTON, 1874–1936

⟡ A LETTER FROM SANTA CLAUS ⟡

Palace of St. Nicholas
In the Moon
Christmas Morning

MY DEAR SUSIE CLEMENS:

I have received and read all the letters which you and your little sister have written me by the hand of your mother and your nurses; I have also read those which you little people have written me with your own hands—for although you did not use any characters that are in grown peoples' alphabet, you used the characters that all children in all lands on earth and in the twinkling stars use; and as all my subjects in the moon are children and use no character but that, you will easily understand that I can read your and your baby sister's jagged and fantastic marks without any trouble at all. But I had trouble with those letters which you dictated through your mother and the nurses, for I am a foreigner and cannot read English writing well. You will find that I made no mistakes about the things which you and the baby ordered in your own letters—I went down your chimney at midnight when you were asleep and delivered them all myself—and kissed both of you, too, because you are good children, well trained, nice mannered, and about the most obedient little people I ever saw.

MARK TWAIN, 1835-1910

⚬⤳ CHRISTMAS PUDDING ⤵⚬

INGREDIENTS.— ½ lb. of beef suet, 2 ozs. of flour, ½ lb. of raisins, ¼ lb. of mixed peel, ½ a grated nutmeg, ½ oz. of mixed spice, ½ oz. of ground cinnamon, 1 gill of milk, 1 wineglassful of rum or brandy, ½ lb. of breadcrumbs, ½ lb. of sultanas, ¼ lb. of currants, 1 lemon, 2 ozs. of desiccated cocoanut or shredded almonds, a pinch of salt, 4 eggs.

METHOD.— Skin the suet and chop it finely. Clean the fruit, stone the raisins, finely shred the mixed peel; peel and chop the lemon-rind. Put all the dry ingredients in a basin and mix well. Add the milk, stir in the eggs one at a time, add the rum or brandy, and the strained juice of the lemon. Work the whole thoroughly for some minutes, so that the ingredients are well blended. Put the mixture in a well-buttered basin or pudding-cloth; if the latter is used it should be buttered or floured. Boil for about 4 hours, or steam for at least 5 hours.

AVERAGE COST.— 1s. 10d. SUFFICIENT for 8 or 9 persons.

MRS BEETON, 1836–1865

⟢ TURKEY, ROASTED ⟢

INGREDIENTS. – 1 turkey, 1 to 2 lbs. of sausage meat, 1 to 1½ lbs. of veal forcemeat, 2 or 3 slices of bacon, 1 pint of good gravy, bread sauce, fat for basting.

METHOD. – Prepare and truss the turkey. Fill the crop with sausage meat, and put the veal forcemeat inside the body of the bird. Skewer the bacon over the breast, baste well with hot fat, and roast in front of a clear fire or in a moderate oven from 1¾ to 2¼ hours, according to age and size of the bird. Baste frequently, and about 20 minutes before serving remove the bacon to allow the breast to brown. Remove the trussing strings, serve on a hot dish, and send the gravy and bread sauce to table in sauce boats.

TIME. – From 1¾ to 2¼ hours. AVERAGE COST, 10s. to 16s. SEASONABLE from September to February.

MRS BEETON, 1836–1865

᎒᎐ **THE GOOSE** ᎒᎐

UCH a bustle ensued that you might have thought a goose the rarest of all birds; a feathered phenomenon, to which a black swan was a matter of course—and in truth it was something very like it in that house. Mrs. Cratchit made the gravy (ready beforehand in a little saucepan), hissing hot; Master Peter mashed the potatoes with incredible vigour; Miss Belinda sweetened up the apple-sauce; Martha dusted the hot plates; Bob took Tiny Tim beside him in a tiny corner at the table; the two young Cratchits set chairs for everybody, not forgetting themselves, and mounting guard upon their posts, crammed spoons into their mouths, lest they should shriek for goose before their turn came to be helped. At last the dishes were set on, and grace was said. It was succeeded by a breathless pause, as Mrs. Cratchit, looking slowly all along the carving-knive, prepared to plunge it in the breast; but when she did, and when the long expected gush of stuffing issued forth, one murmur of delight arose all round the board, and even Tiny Tim, excited by the two young Cratchits, beat on the table with the handle of his knife, and feebly cried Hurrah!

FROM *A CHRISTMAS CAROL* BY CHARLES DICKENS, 1812–1870

᭙ GOD BLESS US EVERY ONE ᭙

ALLO! A great deal of steam! The pudding was out of the copper. A smell like a washing-day! That was the cloth. A smell like an eating-house and a pastrycook's next door to each other, with a laundress's next door to that! That was the pudding! In half a minute Mrs Cratchit entered – flushed, but smiling proudly – with the pudding, like a speckled cannon-ball, so hard and firm, blazing in half of half-a-quartern of ignited brandy, and bedight with Christmas holly stuck into the top.

Oh, a wonderful pudding! Bob Cratchit said, and calmly too, that he regarded it as the greatest success achieved by Mrs Cratchit since their marriage. Mrs Cratchit said that now the weight was off her mind, she would confess she had had her doubts about the quantity of flour. Everybody had something to say about it, but nobody said or thought it was at all a small pudding for a large family. It would have been flat heresy to do so. Any Cratchit would have blushed to hint at such a thing.

At last the dinner was all done, the cloth was cleared, the hearth swept, and the fire made up. The compound in the jug being tasted, and considered perfect, apples and oranges were put upon the table, and a shovel-full of chestnuts on the fire. Then all the Cratchit family drew round the hearth, in what Bob Cratchit called a circle, meaning half a one; and at Bob Cratchit's elbow stood the family display of glass. Two tumblers, and a custard-cup without a handle.

These held the hot stuff from the jug, however, as well as golden goblets would have done; and Bob served it out with beaming looks, while the chestnuts on the fire sputtered and cracked noisily. Then Bob proposed:

"A Merry Christmas to us all, my dears. God bless us!"

Which all the family re-echoed.

"God bless us every one!" said Tiny Tim, the last of all.

FROM *A CHRISTMAS CAROL* BY CHARLES DICKENS, 1812–1870

GABRIEL took his seat boldly at the head of the table and, having looked to the edge of the carver, plunged his fork firmly into the goose. He felt quite at ease now for he was an expert carver and liked nothing better than to find himself at the head of a well-laden table.

"Miss Furlong, what shall I send you?" he asked. "A wing or a slice of the breast?"

"Just a small slice of the breast."

"Miss Higgins, what for you?"

"O, anything at all, Mr Conroy."

While Gabriel and Miss Daly exchanged plates of goose and plates of ham and spiced beef Lily went from guest to guest with a dish of hot floury potatoes wrapped in a white napkin. This was Mary Jane's idea and she had also suggested apple sauce for the goose but Aunt Kate had said that plain roast goose without apple sauce had always been good enough for her and she hoped she might never eat worse. Mary Jane waited on her pupils and saw that they got the best slices and Aunt Kate and Aunt Julia opened and carried across from the piano bottles of stout and ale for the gentlemen and bottles of minerals for the ladies. There was a great deal of confusion and laughter and noise, the noise of orders and counter-orders, of knives and forks, of corks and glass-stoppers. Gabriel began to carve second helpings as soon as he had finished the first round without serving himself. Every one protested loudly so that he compromised by taking a long draught of stout for he had found the carving hot work. Mary Jane settled down quietly to her supper but Aunt Kate and Aunt Julia were still toddling round the table, walking on each other's heels, getting in each other's way and giving each other unheeded orders. Mr Browne begged of them to sit down and eat their suppers and so did Gabriel but they said there was time enough so that, at

last Freddy Malins stood up and, capturing Aunt Kate, plumped her down on her chair amid general laughter.

When everyone had been well served Gabriel said, smiling:

"Now, if anyone wants a little more of what vulgar people call stuffing let him or her speak."

A chorus of voices invited him to begin his own supper and Lily came forward with three potatoes which she had reserved for him.

"Very well," said Gabriel amiably, as he took another preparatory draught, "kindly forget my existence, ladies and gentlemen, for a few minutes."

FROM "THE DEAD" BY JAMES JOYCE, 1882–1941

❦ THE KISSING BUNCH ❦

"GREY rabbit! He's been! Wake up! He's been in the
night!"

"Who?" cried Grey Rabbit, rubbing her eyes and
sitting up in a fright. "Who? Has Rat been?"

"Santa Claus!" cried Hare, capering up and down by
her bed. "Be quick and come downstairs and see the
surprises."

Grey Rabbit dressed hurriedly, but there was a little
twinkle in her eyes as she entered the room.

"Look what he brought me!" cried Squirrel, holding
out a pair of fur mittens and bedroom slippers made from
sheep's wool.

"And he gave me a spotted handkerchief, and a musical
box," cried Hare excitedly, and he turned the handle of
the little round box from which came a jolly tune which
set their feet dancing.

"Look at the Kissing Bunch!" Hare went on. "Isn't it
lovely! Let's all kiss under it."

So they gave their Christmas morning kisses under the
round Christmas Bunch in the time-honoured way.

FROM *LITTLE GREY RABBIT'S CHRISTMAS* BY ALISON UTTLEY, 1884–1976

⟶⟡ MISTLETOE ⟡⟵

SITTING under the mistletoe
(Pale green, fairy mistletoe)
One last candle burning low,
All the sleepy dancers gone,
Just one candle burning on,
Shadows lurking everywhere :
Someone came, and kissed me there.

Tired I was; my head would go
Nodding under the mistletoe
(Pale green, fairy mistletoe)
No footstep came, no voice, but only,
Just as I sat there, sleepy, lonely,
Stooped in the still and shadowy air,
Lips unseen – and kissed me there.

WALTER DE LA MARE, 1873–1956

O LITTLE TOWN OF BETHLEHEM

O LITTLE town of Bethlehem,
How still we see thee lie!
Above thy deep and dreamless sleep
The silent stars go by:
Yet in thy dark street shineth
The everlasting Light;
The hopes and fears of all the years
Are met in thee to-night.

O morning stars, together
Proclaim the holy birth,
And praises sing to God the King,
And peace to men on earth;
For Christ is born of Mary;
And, gathered all above,
While mortals sleep, the angels keep
Their watch of wondering love.

PHILLIPS BROOKS, 1835–1893

⟶⟩⟨⟨ REELING ON ICE ⟩⟩⟨⟵

LD Wardle led the way to a pretty large sheet of ice; and the fat boy and Mr. Weller, having shovelled and swept away the snow which had fallen on it during the night, Mr. Bob Sawyer adjusted his skates with a dexterity which to Mr. Winkle was perfectly marvellous and described circles with his left leg, and cut figures of eight, and inscribed upon the ice, without once stopping for breath, a great many other pleasant and astonishing devices, to the excessive satisfaction of Mr. Pickwick, Mr. Tupman, and the ladies: which reached a pitch of positive enthusiasm, when old Wardle and Benjamin Allen, assisted by the aforesaid Bob Sawyer, performed some mystic evolutions, which they called a reel.

All this time, Mr. Winkle, with his face and hands blue with the cold, had been forcing a gimlet into the soles of his feet, and putting his skates on, with the points behind, and getting the straps into a very complicated and entangled state, with the assistance of Mr. Snodgrass, who knew rather less about skates than a Hindoo. At length, however, with the assistance of Mr. Weller the unfortunate skates were firmly screwed and buckled on, and Mr. Winkle was raised to his feet.

"Now, then, sir," said Sam, in an encouraging tone; "off with you, and show 'em how to do it."

"Stop, Sam, stop!" said Mr. Winkle, trembling violently, and clutching hold of Sam's arms with the grasp of a drowning man. "How slippery it is, Sam."

"Not an uncommon thing upon ice, sir," replied Mr. Weller. "Hold up, sir!"

This last observation of Mr. Weller's bore reference to a demonstration Mr. Winkle made at the instant, of a frantic desire to throw his feet in the air, and dash the back of his head on the ice.

"These—these—are very awkward skates; ain't they, Sam?" inquired Mr. Winkle, staggering.

"I'm afeerd there's a orkard gen'l'm'n in 'em, sir," replied Sam.

"Now, Winkle," cried Mr. Pickwick, quite unconscious that there was anything the matter. "Come; the ladies are all anxiety."

"Yes, yes," replied Mr. Winkle, with a ghastly smile. "I'm coming."

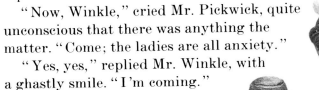

FROM *THE PICKWICK CLUB*
BY CHARLES DICKENS, 1812–1870

⊹❊⊱ HOME FOR CHRISTMAS ⊰❊⊹

THIS is meeting time again. Home is the magnet. The winter land roars and hums with the eager speed of return journeys. The dark is noisy and bright with late-night arrivals–doors thrown open, running shadows on snow, open arms, kisses, voices and laughter, laughter at everything and nothing. Inarticulate, giddying and confused are those original minutes of being back again. The very familiarity of everything acts like shock. Contentment has to be drawn in slowly, steadyingly, in deep breaths–there is so much of it. We rely on home not to change, and it does not, wherefore we give thanks. Again Christmas: abiding point of return. Set apart by its mystery, mood and magic, the season seems in a way to stand outside time. All that is dear, that is lasting, renews its hold on us: we are home again. . . .

FROM *HOME FOR CHRISTMAS* BY ELIZABETH BOWEN, 1899–1973

Acknowledgments

Bridgeman Art Library:
p12–13 Edward Frederick Brewtmall, Warrington Museum & Art Gallery; p14 William Dyce, National Gallery of Scotland; p16 Charles Spencelayh, Private Collection; p19 John William Waterhouse, Manchester City Art Gallery; p23 Henri Gervex, Musée Des Beaux Arts, Bordeaux; p27 John William Waterhouse, Hessisches Landesmuseum, Darnstadt, Germany; p29 Eugene De Blaas, Private Collection; p30–31 Sir Frank Dickset, City of Bristol Museum & Art Gallery; p33 Gustave Klimt, Kunsthistorisches Museum; p35 Jean-Honore Fragonard, Frick Collection, New York; p37 Evelyn De Morgan, De Morgan Foundation; p42 Jules Alexandre Grun, Musée Des Beaux Arts, Tourcoing; p43 Elias Van Den Broeck, Private Collection; p48–49 *The Wedding*: V Marais Milton/Eaton Gallery, London; p51 *Trust Me*: John Everett Millais/Forbes Magazine Collection; p52–53 *Ask Me No More*: Sir Lawrence Alma-Tadema/Private Collection; p56 *At the Window*: Anna Alma-Tadema/Christopher Wood Gallery, London; p59 *A Summer Shower*: Edith Hayllar/Forbes Magazine Collection, NY; p60 *Louis Signorino Seated in his Study*: Gustave Bourgain/Galerie George, London; p61 *Portrait of a Young Woman*: Edmond Francois Aman-Jean/Musée du Petit Palais, Paris; p65 *Till Death Us Do Part*: Edmund Blair Leighton/Forbes Magazine Collection, NY; p66 *Fresh from the Altar*: Jessica Hayllar/Christie's, London; p70–71 *The Only Daughter*: Jessica Hayllar/Forbes Magazine Collection, NY; p73 *La Mondaine*: James Jacques Tissot/Joey & Toby Tanenbaum Collection, Toronto; p74–75 *Signor Marsilio and his Wife*: Lorenzo Lotto/Prado, Madrid; p77 *Au Café*: Fernand Toussanit/Whitford and Hughes, London; p79 *Lady with a Cat*: Charles Massard/Waterhouse and Dodd, London; p85 *The Campanile and the Doge's Palace with St Mark's in the Background*: James R W S Holland/Roy Miles Fine Paintings, London; p86 *Dance at Bougival*: Pierre Auguste Renoir/Museum of Fine Arts, Boston; p90 *Entrance to the Port of Marseilles*: William Callow/Towneley Hall Art Gallery & Museum; p91 *Collioure*: J D Innes/Bradford City Art Gallery & Museums; p92 *The Wanderer*: Casper David Friedrich/Kunsthalle, Hamburg; p93 *An Alpine Lake*: Karl Millner/Christie's, London; p94–95 *A Village Fête in the Rhine Valley*: Jan, the elder Griffier/Johnny Van Haeften Gallery; p100–101 *Lake Como*: Gustave Mascart/Cider House Galleries Ltd, London; p102 *Bridge of Sighs*: William Etty/City of York Art Gallery; p103 *Venice*: Gaston Hippolyte Boucaart/

Gavin Graham Gallery, London; p104–105 *The Campanile and the Doge's Palace with St Mark's in the Background*: James R W S Holland/ Roy Miles Fine Paintings, London; p107 *At the Window*: Hans Heyerdahl/Nasjonal-galleriet, Oslo; p108–109 *Florence*: Andreas Marko/Christie's, London; p110–111 *The Forum, Rome*: Gustav Palm/ Bonham's London; p112–113 *Amalfi*: Carl Frederick Aagaard/Christie's, London; p114 *A Contented Mind's a Continual Feast*: Nicol Erskine/ Harrogate Museums & Art Galleries; p115 *Le Recontre* or *Bonjour M. Courbet* (detail): Gustave Courbet/Musée Fabre Montpellier; p116–117 *One of the People, an Incident in the Life of The Right Honourable William Ewart Gladstone*: Christie's, London; p120 *La Pensée*: Pierre Auguste Renoir/National Gallery of Art, Washington; p122 *Le Berceau*: Berthe Morisot/Louvre, Paris; p124–125 *Day Dreams*: Walter Langley/City of Bristol Museum and Art Gallery; p131 *Maternal Love*: Vincenzo Irolli/Josef Mensing Gallery, Hamm-Rhynern; p132 *Pontus* (detail): Carl Larsson/National Museum, Stockholm; p137 *Sur la Plage* (detail): Charles C J Hoffbauer/Musée de Roubaix/Photographie Giraudon, Paris; p138 *A Morning Stroll*: Dorothea Sharp/Whitford & Hughes, London; p139 *Going to Bed*: John Burgess/Gavin Graham Gallery, London; p142 *An Invitation*: Mary Gow/Christopher Wood Gallery, London; p144–145 *The Music Lesson*: Frederick, Lord Leighton/Guildhall Art Gallery, London; p146–147 *Boys Netting Crabs*: John Bulloch Souter/Roy Miles Fine Paintings, London; p148 *Portrait of a Girl*: Domenico Ghirlandaio/ National Gallery, London; p150 *Portrait of the Artist's Son* (detail): Augustus John/The Fine Art Society, London; p151 *Madame Monet on the Sofa*: Claude Monet/Musée d'Orsay, Paris; p154 *A Fine Vintage*: Gerard Portielje/Private Collection; p155 *Winter Scene*: Anon; p167 *The Nativity*: Gerrit Van Honthorst/Galleria Degli, Uffizi, Florence; p169 *Father Christmas with Children*: Karl Rogers/ Victoria and Albert Museum; p171 *Christmas Turkey*: Sophie Anderson/Private Collection; p173 *The Christmas Hamper*: Robert Braithwaite Martineau/Private Collection; p177 *The Corner of the Table*: Paul Chabas/Musée Des Beaux Arts, Tourcoing/Giraudon; p181 *Our Lady Worshipping the Child*: Antonio Correggio/Galleria Degli, Uffizi, Florence; p185 *Convalescent*: Jules Emile Saintin.

Collins Publishers:
p178 'The Kissing Bunch' illustration by Margaret Tempest.

First published in Great Britain as *Love* in 1988, *The Grand Tour*
in 1991, *Mother and Child* in 1993, and *Christmas* in 1989 by
PAVILION BOOKS LIMITED
London House, Great Eastern Wharf
Parkgate Road, London SW11 4NQ
This edition first published in Great Britain in 1999

Text © Sheila Pickles 1988, 1989, 1991, 1993, 1999
Design and layout © Pavilion Books Ltd. 1999

The moral right of the author has been asserted

Designed by Bernard Higton

A CIP catalogue record for this book is available
from the British Library.

ISBN 1 86205 250 6

Set in DeVinne Roman
Printed and bound in Hong Kong

2 4 6 8 10 9 7 5 3 1

This book can be ordered direct from the publisher.
Please contact the Marketing Department.
But try your bookshop first.